HEARERS
OF THE
WORD

PRAYING & EXPLORING THE READINGS
ADVENT & CHRISTMAS YEAR B

KIERAN J O'MAHONY OSA

Published by Messenger Publications, 2020

ISBN 9781788122849

Designed by Messenger Publications Design Department
Cover Images: collage Shutterstock
Typeset in Adobe Caslon Pro and Adobe Bitter
Printed by Hussar Books

Messenger Publications,
37 Leeson Place, Dublin D02 E5V0
www.messenger.ie

'Hope' is the thing with feathers

'Hope' is the thing with feathers –
That perches in the soul –
And sings the tune without the
words –
And never stops – at all –

And sweetest – in the Gale – is
heard –
And sore must be the storm –
That could abash the little Bird
That kept so many warm –

I've heard it in the chillest land –
And on the strangest Sea –
Yet – never – in Extremity,
It asked a crumb – of me.

Emily Dickinson
(1830–1886)

For my Uncle Joe
and in memory of my Uncle Frank

For in hope we were saved.
Now hope that is seen is not hope,
because who hopes for what he sees?
But if we hope for what we do not see,
we eagerly wait for it with endurance.
(Romans 8:24–25)

Table of Contents

Introduction

ADVENT opens the door to hope. One of strengths of the liturgical year is the summons to inhabit again different dimensions of the Christian proclamation. Historically, Advent would have been seen as a penitential season akin to Lent but, in reality, it is a joy-filled season of preparation. Today, more than ever, we need to hear the message of hope and joy.

Our great companion in this season is the book of the prophet Isaiah. On three of the Sundays of Advent, we hear from him, as well as on Christmas Day (all four Masses) and on the Epiphany. Even more richly, Isaiah is our constant companion in the daily readings. Isaiah is worth befriending (a reading list is to be found at the end of this book). So much early Christian vocabulary and imagery are taken from him that Isaiah was sometimes known as the Fifth Gospel. Even more, the poetry is some of the very best in the Hebrew Bible. Who can resist the delight and surprise of words like these?

> For the sake of Zion I will not be silent;
> for the sake of Jerusalem I will not be quiet,
> until her vindication shines brightly
> and her deliverance burns like a torch.

> Nations will see your vindication,
> and all kings your splendour.
> You will be called by a new name
> that the LORD himself will give you.
> You will be a majestic crown in the hand of the LORD,
> a royal turban in the hand of your God.

> You will no longer be called, 'Abandoned',
> and your land will no longer be called 'Desolate'.
> Indeed, you will be called 'My Delight is in Her',
> and your land 'Married'.

> For the LORD will take delight in you,
> and your land will be married to him.
>
> As a young man marries a young woman,
> so your sons will marry you.
> As a bridegroom rejoices over a bride,
> so your God will rejoice over you. (Isaiah 62:1–5 NET)

As indicated regularly in the notes, it is has long been recognised that 'Isaiah' is really three poet-prophets writing at quite distinct times. Even so, the divisions into 1–39, 40–55 and 56–66 are not so neat. There is a consistent picture of God across the text and the final editor(s) made sure the text as it stands reads well without too many jolts. Like all the prophets, Isaiah declares to us what we are unwilling or unable to hear. In the readings chosen for Advent, both Second and Third Isaiah call us to hope-filled joy. As we stumble our way through a pandemic, it is easy to be overwhelmed by the negative and correspondingly hard to hear the Good News. A much later prophet, Paul, puts it like this:

> But as God is faithful, our message to you is not 'Yes' and 'No'.
> For the Son of God, Jesus Christ, the one who was proclaimed among you by us – by me and Silvanus and Timothy – was not 'Yes' and 'No', but it has always been 'Yes' in him. For every one of God's promises are 'Yes' in him; therefore also through him the 'Amen' is spoken, to the glory we give to God. (2 Corinthians 1:18–20)

Both hope and joy are marks of freedom, of the deep inner freedom of the heart. This freedom is not 'cheap grace', accessed by some natural effervescence. On the contrary, Christian joy and Christian hope spring from our encounter with Jesus the Christ and from living the Good News. It is not an accident that Pope Francis combines his invitation to the joy of the Gospel with his invitation to a renewed personal encounter with Jesus. The opening words of *The Joy of the Gospel* still speak today:

The joy of the gospel fills the hearts and lives of all who encounter Jesus. Those who accept his offer of salvation are set free from sin, sorrow, inner emptiness and loneliness. With Christ joy is constantly born anew. In this Exhortation I wish to encourage the Christian faithful to embark upon a new chapter of evangelisation marked by this joy, while pointing out new paths for the Church's journey in years to come. (*The Joy of the Gospel*, 1).

The Scriptures are our privileged place of encounter, a kind of Sacrament of the Word. If we open our ears, our hearts and our lives, God will speak to us through the Holy Readings. In the happy phrase of St Francis de Sales, *cor ad cor loquitur*, heart speaks to heart (in a letter of 1614).

Prayer before reading Scripture

God of the silent cosmos, we wait as hearers of the word.

You offer us the word of life: *speak, Lord, your servants are listening.*

You call us to conversion: *may your word penetrate our hearts and change our lives.*

You invite us to generous joy-filled service: *may the Scriptures be our constant companion.*

This we ask through Christ our Lord. Amen.

The pointers for prayer on the Gospel readings are almost all by my confrère, John Byrne OSA.

Chapter 1

Advent 1B

Thought for the day

Beginning again is an invitation to look in two directions, a Janus-like experience, as we face two ways. What happened for me in the last year, both in my ordinary life and in my life as a believer, a person of faith? For what do I ask forgiveness? For what do I give thanks? We also look forward and the new beginning gives us a chance to start again on the way of discipleship. Both thanksgiving and renewal are to be found in today's readings. The gospel is in invitation to wake up, to keep watch, to live fully the present moment under God, in whom we live and move and have our being. Amen.

Prayer

Wake us up, O God, and rouse us from the slumber of the everyday that we may recognise you in every moment and in every person, today and every day of our lives. Through Christ our Lord. Amen.

🌿 Gospel 🌿

Mk 13:32 *'But about that day or hour no one knows, neither the angels in heaven, nor the Son, but only the Father.'*

³³ [Jesus said:] 'Beware, keep alert; for you do not know when the time will come. ³⁴ It is like a man going on a journey, when he leaves home and puts his slaves in charge, each with his work, and commands the doorkeeper to be on the watch. ³⁵ Therefore, keep awake – for you do not know when the

master of the house will come, in the evening, or at midnight, or at cockcrow, or at dawn, [36] or else he may find you asleep when he comes suddenly. [37] And what I say to you I say to all: Keep awake.'

Initial observations

In the narrative of Mark, chapter 13 stands between Jesus' presence and disputations in Jerusalem (chapters 11–12) and the Passion Narrative (chapters 14–16). Chapter 13 is often called the Markan Apocalypse or the Little Apocalypse. The lectionary omits v. 32 but it is included here because it makes for a more natural introduction to the warnings. If even the Son does not know, then a fortiori the disciples need to be on the watch.

The writing here is apocalyptic, which requires very careful handling (see below). Apart from that, the threatening tone could grate on our ears today. In general, apocalyptic is meant to be neither a prophecy nor a description of the future. It interprets the present and tries to promote fidelity and steadfastness. Mark, written perhaps during the Jewish War (AD 66–73), is facing three situations: (i) it is probable that the communities for which the gospel was written had experienced tribulation of some kind, with the consequent temptation to give up; (ii) complacency engendered by the apparent delay in Jesus' return; (iii) feverish identification of the signs of the end. For Mark, the tribulations are the birth pangs of the end; his teaching is an invitation to be both steadfast and alert.

In Mark's narrative, the location is the Mount of Olives in view of the Temple (Mark 11:11, 15–16, 27; 12:35); the topic takes up issues anticipated by Jesus' arrival in the Temple (11:1–10) and his judgement of it (12:1–11); the audience – Jesus, Peter, James, John and Andrew – reminds us of the opening scene of the Galilean ministry (1:16–20).

Kind of writing

This is written in apocalyptic language. The best Old Testament example is the book of Daniel and the best New Testament example is the Apocalypse, the book of Revelation. In general, an apocalypse interprets the present and, so to speak, 'names the times we live in'. On foot of the description, certain attitudes or actions are taught, to help us live these times in an authentic way. The great virtues are steadfastness (stickability!) and watchfulness.

Old Testament background

The biblical background for Mark 13 as a whole is the book of Daniel 7–12.

> As I watched in the night visions, I saw one like a human being coming with the clouds of heaven. And he came to the Ancient One and was presented before him. To him was given dominion and glory and kingship, that all peoples, nations, and languages should serve him. His dominion is an everlasting dominion that shall not pass away, and his kingship is one that shall never be destroyed. (Daniel 7:13–14)

New Testament foreground

(i) Context in Mark: it may help to notice that there are good links between all of chapter 13 and (a) the initial preaching of Jesus in Mark 1:14; (b) the proclamation of the Kingdom in parables in Mark 4:1–34; and (c) the prayer of Jesus in Gethsemane in Mark 14:32–42.

(ii) Mark 13 itself: the evangelist has gathered together disparate items of Jesus' teaching. It is likely that a certain amount of grouping of sayings had already taken place. We may notice some of the following similar themes:
   (a) Sayings on the distress of Israel: 13:14–18,19–20
   (b) Sayings on the distress of the Church: 13:9–13
   (c) Sayings on pseudo–messiahs and the true Messiah: 13:21, 14–16
   (d) Sayings on the the second coming (the *parousia*) and watchfulness: 13:26–27, 34–36

Mark was writing at the time of the Jewish war with the Romans and end-time expectations were really high, in Palestine and elsewhere. He may have gathered together the statements of Jesus for the community at that time, to maintain alertness of spirit and to warn against potential false messiahs and the like. In its present state the chapter falls naturally into the following sections:

    (1) vv. 1–4, Introduction – prophecy of the Temple's doom and the disciples' question;

    (2) vv. 5–23, the Tribulation of Israel and of the Church;

    (3) vv. 24–27, the *parousia* of the Son of Man and the Gathering of the People of God;

    (4) vv. 28–37, the Times of Fulfilment and Exhortations to Watchfulness.

Our excerpt comes from the very last section, inculcating certain attitudes for the present moment, the time of trial. It thus makes a bridge with the feast of Christ the King, which closed the previous liturgical year, and invites us into the new year and the season of Advent, with a tone of expectation, hope and preparation.

St Paul

1 Thessalonians 4:15–5:11 is very close to the atmosphere of Mark 13. It is a little too long to quote, so here is a shorter similar passage from Romans:

> And do this because we know the time, that it is already the hour for us to awake from sleep, for our salvation is now nearer than when we became believers. The night has advanced towards dawn; the day is near. So then we must lay aside the works of darkness, and put on the weapons of light. Let us live decently as in the daytime, not in carousing and drunkenness, not in sexual immorality and sensuality, not in discord and jealousy. Instead, put on the Lord Jesus Christ, and make no provision for the flesh to arouse its desires. (Romans 13:11–14)

Brief commentary

(V.32)

Some of the force of the warning comes from the Son himself not knowing. Of course, this is a surprise to us today. However, there is preparation in Mark 10:40. Furthermore, since the early Christians tended to underline and even increase Jesus' knowledge, this saying is most likely original, in some form, to Jesus himself. In later theological disputes, the Arians used this text against the affirmation of Jesus as true divine and truly human, as defined at the Council of Nicea (AD 325).

(V.33)

Mark is teaching 'watchfulness', conscious living and engagement. It is a frequent idea in this chapter (vv. 5, 9 and 23). 'Watch' makes the necessary connection with Gethsemane and the destiny of Jesus.

(V.34)

This little parable gives a very ordinary, everyday example and has a tendency to allegory: the man on the journey represents the Lord; the slaves/servants stand for the believers; the doorkeeper could be any disciple, with the special duty of watchfulness; the return of the master points to the Second Coming.

(V.35)

The final expansion spells it out very clearly, naming the potential times when the master may return. Mark, interestingly, uses the Roman divisions of the hours of the day, a clue to the world of reference of the community.

(V.36)

Sleep is commonly used to mean inattention, lack of alertness, as well as death. 'Suddenly' adds intensity to the sense of threat involved.

(V.37)

This is the last sentence of the Little Apocalypse and makes for a resounding conclusion, addressed explicitly to each and to all. Watch is taken up again in the next chapter: 14:34, 37, 38.

Today we cannot excite artificially the feverish expectation of the early Christians. We probably do not want to threaten people either.

Nevertheless, the culture is a culture of distraction and it promotes unconscious living, inviting us to live on the surface and to be happy with the merely material. Perhaps there is an entry there for the teaching of this passage and the prayer below may help. We are not intended to sleepwalk through life!

Pointers for prayer

a) The coming of the master is not just the moment of death, but any moment of grace. Recall unexpected graces – good things that happened when they were not anticipated.

b) Recall times when you were particularly alert and aware of what was going on in you and around you, and then contrast that with moments when such alertness and awareness were not present.

c) The servants were given charge of the household, 'each with their own job'. Identify with the servants as people given a responsibility within the household of God's people. What has it been like for you when you have been shown trust in this way by another person? What is it like for you to see yourself trusted in this way by God?

d) Recall your experience of good 'doorkeepers', people who were there and ready to receive you even when you came at an awkward or unexpected time. Think also about your experience of being a good 'doorkeeper' for another.

e) Jesus says that what he is saying to his disciples he is saying to all. Have there been times when you have been a messenger of hope to others, encouraging them to wait for a moment of grace? Who have been the ones to encourage you?

Prayer

Rend the heavens and come down, O God of all the ages!
Rouse us from sleep, deliver us from our heedless ways, and form us into a
watchful people, that, at the advent of your Son,
he may find us doing what is right, mindful of all you command.

Grant this through him, whose coming is certain, whose day draws near,
your Son, our Lord Jesus Christ, who lives and reigns with you
in the unity of the Holy Spirit, God for ever and ever. Amen.

🌿 Second Reading 🌿

1 Cor 1:1 *From Paul, called to be an apostle of Christ Jesus by the will of God, and Sosthenes, our brother,* [2] *to the church of God that is in Corinth, to those who are sanctified in Christ Jesus, and called to be saints, with all those in every place who call on the name of our Lord Jesus Christ, their Lord and ours.* [3] Grace and peace to you from God our Father and the Lord Jesus Christ!

[4] I always thank my God for you because of the grace of God that was given to you in Christ Jesus. [5] For you were made rich in every way in him, in all your speech and in every kind of knowledge – [6] just as the testimony about Christ has been confirmed among you – [7] so that you do not lack any spiritual gift as you wait for the revelation of our Lord Jesus Christ. [8] He will also strengthen you to the end, so that you will be blameless on the day of our Lord Jesus Christ. [9] God is faithful, by whom you were called into fellowship with his son, Jesus Christ our Lord.

Initial observations

In Advent, all three readings focus on the same topic, so today, with Paul, we reflect on the end of time, the last days. Paul mentions the 'revelation of our Lord Jesus Christ', the 'end', and the 'day of our Lord Jesus Christ.' The faithfulness of God is also a key part of that apocalyptic worldview. Vv. 1–2 (added above) complete the greeting.

Kind of writing

(i) This is a thanksgiving, present in all Paul's letters except Galatians. He uses the thanksgiving to gain the attention, good will and receptivity of the Corinthians, by praying for them and by praising their strengths (which, it turns out, can also be their weaknesses!).

(ii) At the same time, this passage displays Paul as an apocalyptic Jew of the first century. Apocalyptic is a term used to describe both a kind of writing and a worldview. Central to this worldview is the hope in God's faithfulness and consequent belief in the resurrection, however that may be imagined. The term apocalyptic and the worldview may seem foreign to us. However, it is a response to *the* question present in all faiths: how to continue believing in God with so much evil and suffering in the world.

Origin of the reading

It is known that Paul was in Corinth in the winter of AD 51 and the spring of 52. The letter is long because there are major issues in the Corinthian community, some of which are hinted at in this introductory thanksgiving. For example, he mentions competitiveness over the spiritual gifts (ch. 12–14) and their inability to believe or imagine that all will rise with Christ at the end (ch. 15).

Related passage

> But now Christ has been raised from the dead, the first fruits of those who have fallen asleep. For since death came through a man, the resurrection of the dead also came through a man. For just as in Adam all die, so also in Christ all will be made alive. But each in his own order: Christ, the first fruits; then when Christ comes, those who belong to him. Then comes the end, when he hands over the kingdom to God the Father, when he has brought to an end all rule and all authority and power. For he must reign until he has put all his enemies under his feet. The last enemy to be eliminated is death. (1 Corinthians 15:20–26)

Brief commentary

(V. 3)

The greeting is pointed to the specific needs in Corinth: *grace* because all is gift, *peace* because of rivalry. Some Corinthians gave themselves a higher status, in their own minds, because of the more extrovert spiritual gifts.

(V. 4)

This typical introductory line is replicated elsewhere (1 Thessalonians 1:2; Romans 1:3 etc.). To know that someone prays for you is very heart-warming. However, even at the start, Paul already anticipates the idea that their gifts are *not* their own, but come through the grace *of God*.

(V. 5)

This is especially true in Corinth, where the spiritual gifts are evidently abundant *and prized*. For Paul's considered reply, see chapters 12–14.

(V. 6)

Why does he mention 'testimony'? The noun is rare in Paul (only here and in 2 Corinthians 1:12), while the verb is more common (Romans 3:21; 10:2; 1 Corinthians 15:15; 2 Corinthians 8:3; Galatians 4:15). It is possibly because in this letter Paul draws down the teaching *tradition* to remind the Corinthians. See the Lord's Supper in 11:23–26 and the resurrection creed in 15:3–5.

(V. 7)

Notice that the spiritual gifts, to which they are so attached, are not intended to last for ever. On the contrary, as we read further on: *But as for prophecies, they will come to an end; as for tongues, they will cease; as for knowledge, it will come to an end.* (1 Corinthians 13:8). Instead, they are given *with a view to the end*, the revealing (literally the *apocalypse*) of Jesus. The end includes the resurrection of the body, a teaching that was difficult even then for some in the community.

(V. 8)

Again, we notice that this strengthening is gift in view of what will happen at the end of time. It is implied – none too subtly – that the Corinthians need help to become/remain blameless.

(V. 9)

The faithfulness of God is a key teaching of apocalyptic in general and Paul in particular. See Romans 3:21–26 in the NET translation. Again, the comment on fellowship (*koinōnia*; Romans 15:26; 1 Corinthians 1:9; 10:16; 2 Corinthians 6:14; 8:4; 9:13; 13:13; Galatians 2:9; Philippians 1:5; 2:1; 3:10; Philemon 1:6) is at the heart of a Paul's teaching, yet critically missing in Corinth.

Pointers for prayer

a) Looking at your own community of faith and, indeed, your being part of it, for what do you give thanks? What are the gifts God has bestowed on the community as a whole and on the individuals within it?

b) We are called into fellowship with others. Can I name what I receive as part of that fellowship and give thanks? Can I say – humbly! – what I bring to our fellowship?

c) God is faithful. Perhaps at this point in my life, I need to be reminded of that? Perhaps I need to look at my own faithfulness and how I live it?

Prayer

Faithful God, stay with us on the journey that we try to be faithful just as you are faithful, so that on the day of Lord Jesus Christ you may welcome us into fellowship with all the saints. Grant this through Christ our Lord. Amen.

🌿 First Reading 🌿

Is 63:16 For you are our father, though Abraham does not know us and Israel does not acknowledge us; you, O LORD, are our father; our Redeemer from of old is your name. ¹⁷ Why, O LORD, do you make us stray from your ways and harden our heart, so that we do not fear you? Turn back for the sake of your servants, for the sake of the tribes that are your heritage.

¹⁸ *Your holy people took possession for a little while;*
but now our adversaries have trampled down your sanctuary.
¹⁹ *We have long been like those whom you do not rule,*
like those not called by your name.

Isaiah 64:1 O that you would tear open the heavens and come down, so that the mountains would quake at your presence. ² as when fire kindles brushwood and the fire causes water to boil, to make your name known to your adversaries, so that the nations might tremble at your presence! ³ When you did awesome deeds that we did not expect, you came down, the mountains quaked at your presence. ⁴ From ages past no one has heard, no ear has perceived, no eye has seen any God besides you, who works for those who wait for him. ⁵ You meet those who gladly do right, those who remember you in your ways. But you were angry, and we sinned; because you hid yourself we transgressed. ⁶ We have all become like one who is unclean, and all our righteous deeds are like a filthy cloth. We all fade like a leaf, and our iniquities, like the wind, take us away. ⁷ There is no one who calls on your name, or attempts to take hold of you; for you have hidden your face from us, and have delivered us into the hand of our iniquity. ⁸ Yet, O Lord, you are our Father; we are the clay, and you are our potter; we are all the work of your hand.

Initial observations

This is a very heartfelt prayer, expressing considerable distress, at a time when people were wondering (not for the last time) where God is in all of this.

Kind of writing

The writing is typical of biblical poetry this time in the form of a psalm of lament, running from Isaiah 63:7 to 64:12. Again, the poetry can be enjoyed for its technique of saying things twice. Notice the relationship, for example, between these pairs of lines (parallelism, technically):

> 63:17 Why, O Lord, do you make us stray from your ways
> *and harden our heart, so that we do not fear you?*

The second line often goes a bit deeper, into the cause of the straying: they did not ever fear/respect God, not to mention pray to him.

> 64:7 There is no one who calls on your name, or *attempts to*
> *take hold of you.*

Again, the second line goes deeper: they are not even trying!

The lectionary excerpt has a frame, at the start and at the end: 'You are our Father.' This initial title expands into a wonderful description of God and those who believe in God. Notice that there are two panes or dimensions each time.

GOD	ISRAEL
Lord, redeemer from of old, the liberator God of the Exodus (64:1–4), without equal, the potter.	God's servants, the tribe of God's heritage, those who wait for him, those who do right and remember God's way.
God made them stray and hardened their hearts; God was angry and hid himself; God hid his face and delivered them to their enemies.	They strayed and no longer feared God; they sinned and transgressed; filth and unclean, faded like a leaf; iniquitous; no one calls on God.

The surprise in all this is that it is *God* who is invited to 'convert'!! God has to take some of the blame and the hope is that he will let his true self be seen again. The Hebrew word for 'turn' is *shuv*, and the range of meanings includes to turn around, to repent, to bring back, to refresh. When used of God it means to become devoted once more. It shows a certain courage to address God in such language.

Origin of the reading

Second Isaiah (ch. 40–55) was written during the Babylonian Exile (587–539 BC) and Third Isaiah (ch. 56–66) after the return from Exile. The omitted verses 18 and 19 give us to understand that this prayer was written *after* the return from Exile but *before* the rebuilding of the Temple. It was a time of hopes dashed and not at all unlike later historical moments in the life of the Church.

Related passages

> Woe to you who strive with your Maker, earthen vessels with the potter! Does the clay say to the one who fashions it, 'What are you making'? or 'Your work has no handles'? (Isaiah 45:9)

> Like clay in the hand of the potter, to be moulded as he pleases, so all are in the hand of their Maker, to be given whatever he decides. (Sirach 33:13)

> Has the potter no right over the clay, to make out of the same lump one object for special use and another for ordinary use? (Romans 9:21)

Brief commentary

(V. 16)

Abraham, Isaac and Jacob (=Israel) are the physical 'fathers', but God is the real father of his people. It is strange to imagine Israel not recognising Israel. The writer does not hesitate to call God back to his previous role and reputation. The next verse goes much further.

(V. 17)

God is, in part, blamed for the present painful experience. The Exile was read as a punishment for their own infidelity, but a punishment, nevertheless, *from God*. Verse 17cd is arresting: Turn back for the sake of your servants, for the sake of the tribes that are your heritage. To turn back is an Old Testament expression for conversion. Regularly and rightly the prophets proclaim to the people conversion of heart. Here, by contrast, it is God who is called to contrition and conversion.

(V. 1)

The echo of the covenant on Mount Sinai is a call to God to be faithful to that covenant. The heavens are to be 'torn' because of God's energy and commitment.

(V. 2)

The images used suggest that it is or should be in the nature of God to act, just as fire kindles brushwood etc. God's reputation is at stake: having acted in bringing the people back, he should go the next step and cause them to flourish, if only for the sake of his own name.

(V. 3)

Again the covenant on Sinai is evoked. 'We did not expect' points to the grace, the *unearned and unexpected grace*, the gift of the Exodus.

(V. 4)

The reader notices the use of senses (hearing and seeing), pointing here to the otherness and the uniqueness of God. The description of the faithful as 'those who wait' sets up an expectation that God will finally do something.

(V. 5)

The first two lines are positive; the second two negative. Here we have a summary of Exilic spirituality: infidelity and punishment, but *not* in that order. The emphasis does not fall on the guilt of the people but on the anger of the deity who *caused them to sin*. One could view this as brave and audacious, but also as impertinent and impudent … but then that is how children sometimes relate to their fathers and mothers, with a kind of cheeky overstatement.

(V. 6)

The author offers us a graphic description of the present decline and instability, using two sets of imagery, the purity practices (ritual uncleanness) and nature (autumn leaves). Either way, the faithful are pitifully reduced.

(V. 7)

Again, the first two lines describe the state of things, while the second two lines pinpoint the cause. Continuing in the previous vein, the blame is laid at the door of God, *who has hidden himself.* And again, God's self-regard and reputation (vanity?) are evoked as motives for action.

(V. 8)
This an echo the second creation story in Genesis 2–3 and many other places in the Bible (see the related passages above). The tone is one of resigned devotion: this is who we are and, more importantly, this is who you (God) are! In the whole prayer, we are quite far from saccharine piety, typical of many strands of Christianity. Instead, we are in the world of robust Israelite confidence in God.

Pointers for prayer

a) Believers often long for a more tangible presence of God, a God who comes to meet us. What has been my experience of waiting for God?

b) Clay can be made into many things (see Romans 9:21). How open am I to God's creativity in my own pilgrimage of faith?

Prayer

God, our loving father, when we are absent from you and when you seem absent to us, come again, be close to us, and let us know your presence and action in our lives. We place ourselves in your hands: we are the clay, you the potter. We make our prayer through Christ our Lord. Amen.

Themes across the readings

As for Christmas, Lent and Eastertide, the readings for Advent are usually on the same theme or topic. (This is not the case the rest of the year.) Here is a 'map' of the Advent readings for Year B.

ADVENT READINGS				THEMES
Advent 1	Isaiah 63:16–17; 64:1, 3–8	1 Corinthians 1:3–9	Mark 13:33–37	End of Time
Advent 2	Isaiah 40:1–5, 9–11	2 Peter 3:8–14	Mark 1:1–8	John the Baptist
Advent 3	Isaiah 61:1–2, 10–11	1 Thessalonians 5:16–24	John 1:6–8, 19–28	John the Baptist
Advent 4	2 Samuel 7:1–5, 8–11,16	Romans 16:25–27	Luke 1:26–38	Mary

For the first Sunday of Advent, to be honest, the Old Testament reading doesn't quite fit the gospel as neatly as usual. Vv. 3–5 come closest, with the tone of not expecting and still waiting. How the waiting should unfold is found in v. 5: by doing what is right, remembering God's ways, in some fashion corresponding to the Gospel message 'to stay awake'. There is a somewhat better fit between the gospel and the second reading.

Chapter 2

Advent 2B

Thought for the day

As Christmas approaches, we could ask ourselves: how can we prepare to celebrate the birthday of our Saviour? The proclamation of John the Baptist points to the preparation that really counts: conversion of heart and life. The deeper meaning of *metanoia* is a change of vision, a radically new outlook, in the light of the Gospel. God is our compassionate father, our Abba, who desires nothing less than our hearts, our whole selves. We are accepted and loved by him, while we are still sinners (Romans 5:8). Receiving his forgiving love means a revolution in values, beliefs and direction in life. What else is Christmas about?

Prayer

Loving God, as we your children prepare to celebrate the birth of Jesus our Saviour, help us to prepare our hearts too. May the coming birth of the Son of David encourage us to true repentance and genuine conversion of heart. Through Christ our Lord. Amen.

🌿 Gospel 🌿

Mk 1:1 The beginning of the good news of Jesus Christ, the Son of God.

² As it is written in the prophet Isaiah, 'See, I am sending my messenger ahead of you, who will prepare your way; ³ the voice of one crying out in the wilderness: 'Prepare the way of the Lord, make his paths straight.' ⁴ John the baptiser appeared

in the wilderness, proclaiming a baptism of repentance for the forgiveness of sins. [5] And people from the whole Judean countryside and all the people of Jerusalem were going out to him, and were baptised by him in the River Jordan, confessing their sins. [6] Now John was clothed with camel's hair, with a leather belt around his waist, and he ate locusts and wild honey. [7] He proclaimed, 'The one who is more powerful than I is coming after me; I am not worthy to stoop down and untie the thong of his sandals.[8] I have baptised you with water; but he will baptise you with the Holy Spirit.'

Initial observations

All beginnings are important and this is true in a special way for the four gospels, each of which offers a kind of overture, richly resonant of the themes to come. Matthew opens with the genealogy of Jesus, reflecting his interest in the (dis)continuity with Judaism. Luke writes as a historian and offers us the principles and motives behind his research before embarking on the rest of the first two chapters. John 1:1–18 makes the most remarkable opening, poetic and theological, and at the same time echoing the very first words of the Bible (and this may be a resumption in a different mode of the start of Mark). In this gospel, the opening sentence functions as a *title*, an *introduction* and a *plan* of the gospel (which divides into two parts: 1–8 exploring *messiah*, and 9–16 exploring *Son of God*).

It is also the case that each of the gospels makes a special effort to locate John the Baptist and his ministry as *preparatory* for the coming of Jesus. The fact that throughout the first century you had followers of John the Baptist (they still exist today as the Mandaeans) gave rise to notable anxiety in the Christian movement. It was always possible for the continuing Baptist movement to declare its superiority over Christianity because (a) John had been Jesus' mentor and (b) John had baptised Jesus. The 'one who has' gives to the 'one who has not'! For these reasons, the gospel writers go to some lengths to make sure the reader spots the relative inferiority of John the Baptist in relation to Jesus the

Messiah. For us today, this is a battle long past but it does, nevertheless, help account for some features of the text as it has come down to us.

Kind of writing

The opening verses are an introduction, technically an *exordium*, the function of which is to get the reader's attention and good will and to invite the reader 'in' by anticipating aspects of the story to come. Three steps are taken. The first (v. 1) is a kind of title and programme, as noted above. The second (vv. 2–3) anticipates the narrative with a powerful interpretive lens, that of the Old Testament. In a word, the story to follow is one of fulfilment and continuity. Only after these first two moments do we arrive at the third step, taking us to a particular historical place and personage, the Judean wilderness and John the 'immerser'. It is not without significance that the 'baptiser' immediately points beyond himself to another personage.

Old Testament background

(i) Though not so obvious as John 1:1, Mark 1:1 may echo the very start of the Bible as such in Genesis 1:1. The implication is that this beginning is as important as the very beginning of creation itself.

(ii) 'Good News' as an expression occurs in the Greek Old Testament but nearly always as a *verb* (1 Samuel 31:9; 2 Samuel 1:20; 4:10; 18:19–20, 26, 31; 1 Kings 1:42; 1 Chronicles 10:9; Psalm 39:10; 67:12; 95:2; Wisdom 11:1; Joel 3:5; Nahum 2:1; Isaiah 40:9; 52:7; 60:6; 61:1; Jeremiah 20:15; the *noun* occurs only in 2 Samuel 4:10, in a disturbing context). Isaiah makes the links between 'good news' and the kingdom in this verse:

> How beautiful upon the mountains are the feet of the messenger who announces peace, who brings *good news*, who announces *salvation*, who says to Zion, 'Your God *reigns*.' (Isaiah 52:7)

(iii) 'Messiah' means anointed, and is used of kings, priests and prophets. There is no clear occurrence, in the Hebrew Bible, of 'messiah' meaning a future agent of salvation. For that, we need to turn to the Jewish writings outside the Old Testament, for example the Dead Sea Scrolls, the Psalms of Solomon or the Testaments of the Twelve Patriarchs. The New Testament presumes that many people were looking for a deliverer, a messiah.

(iv) Mark says his citation comes from Isaiah, but in reality he has combined two sources, which are: 'See, I am sending my messenger to prepare the way before me, and the Lord whom you seek will suddenly come to his temple. The messenger of the covenant in whom you delight – indeed, he is coming, says the Lord of hosts' (Malachi 3:1). 'A voice cries out: "In the wilderness prepare the way of the Lord, make straight in the desert a highway for our God"' (Isaiah 40:3).

The attentive reader will notice the shift from 'me' to 'you' in Malachi and the change in punctuation from 'A voice cries out "In the wilderness …" to 'A voice cries out in the wilderness: "Prepare a way …". In a very practical sense, there is no point in crying out in the wilderness because no one will hear you.

(v) It was expected that the end would be ushered in by the appearance of two figures or types, a prophet like Moses (Deuteronomy 18:15) and the return of Elijah (Malachi 4:5). Mark identifies John as 'Elijah' by echoing another Old Testament text: 'They answered him, "A hairy man, with a leather belt around his waist." He said, "It is Elijah the Tishbite"'(2 Kings 1:8).

New Testament foreground

(i) This is preparatory to the baptism of Jesus by John. The baptism is one of the surest facts in early Christianity because it was uncomfortable for the writers to recall it, so they would not have made it up. Jesus was a follower of the Baptist, took baptism from him (Mark 1:9–11) and started his own proclamation, according to Mark, only when his mentor has been imprisoned and effectively silenced (Mark 1:14).

(ii) The first half of this gospel is marked by attempts to grasp the identity of Jesus and comes to a first conclusion in the confession of

Peter at Caesarea Philippi (Mark 8:27–30).

(iii) The proclamation of the Gospel, the good news of the kingdom, is fundamental to the story being proclaimed (Mark 1:1, 14–15; 4:11, 26, 30; 9:1, 47; 10:14–15, 23–25, 29; 12:34; 13:10; 14:9, 25; 15:43; 16:15, 20). The opening proclamation says it all:

'Now after John was arrested, Jesus came to Galilee, proclaiming the good news of God, and saying, "The time is fulfilled, and the kingdom of God has come near; repent, and believe in the good news."'(Mark 1:14–15)

(iv) John is later beheaded (Mark 6:17–29) and, in Mark 11:27–30, the evangelist gives us Jesus' own estimate of John.

St Paul

But how are they to call on one in whom they have not believed? And how are they to believe in one of whom they have never heard? And how are they to hear without someone to proclaim him? And how are they to proclaim him unless they are sent? As it is written, 'How beautiful are the feet of those who bring good news!' (Romans 10:14–15).

Brief commentary

Much of the comment is already present in the remarks above.

(V. 1)
'Beginning', the very first word in Greek, without the article, has three functions: the start of the book, the inauguration of the ministry, the in-breaking of the coming of the kingdom. 'Messiah' is found in all early manuscripts, while 'son of God' is missing in significant early sources.

(Vv. 2–3)
Mark seems to be the first to come up with these citations to help recognise the role of John. The success of this innovation can be seen in John 1:22–23, where the Baptist himself cites Isaiah about himself!

(V. 4)
By means of location in the wilderness, John is shown aligning himself

with those unhappy with the Temple and its cult, such as the Qumran sectarians. Repentance is better rendered conversion and corresponds to the Old Testament to turn or to return to God. It is first of all a positive change, looking to the future, which at another level will certainly include regret for the past.

(V. 5)

Even though the response is clearly beefed up, the popularity of John helps to account, in part, for the need to eliminate him. The account of John's death in Josephus is more plausible than the colourful tale of the dancing girl in Mark 6:14–27. See his *Antiquities of the Jews* 18:116–119. Herod feared that John's popularity might trigger an insurrection.

(V. 6)

John is portrayed as the expected Elijah. Three biblical texts are helpful here. 'On that day the prophets will be ashamed, every one, of their visions when they prophesy; they will not put on *a hairy mantle* in order to deceive' (Zechariah 13:4). 'They answered him, "A hairy man, with a *leather belt* around his waist." He said, "It is Elijah the Tishbite"' (2 Kings 1:8). 'These you may eat from them: the *locust* of any kind, the bald *locust* of any kind, the cricket of any kind, the grasshopper of any kind' (Leviticus 11:22). In this last citation, the latter-day Elijah keeps the dietary laws.

(Vv. 7–8)

It is relatively unlikely that the historical John referenced the Holy Spirit so clearly in the context of immersion/baptism. The Q form of this preaching, preserved in Matthew and Luke, may have looked like this:

> *I baptise you ≤in≥ water, but the one to come after me is more powerful than I, whose sandals I am not fit to ≤take off≥. He will baptise you in ≤holy≥ Spirit and fire.* (Q 3:16b = Matthew 3:11)

The original contrast may have been between water on the one hand, a sign of life, and wind (= *pneuma*) and fire on the other hand, symbols of harvest and judgement. At Mark's hand, the wind becomes the divine Spirit (*pneuma*). The early Christian experience and understanding of baptism may have influenced the telling.

Pointers for prayer

a) John the Baptist is presented as a messenger to prepare the way for Jesus. Who have been messengers to you, preparing the way for the Lord? To whom have you been such a messenger?

b) The voice cries in 'the desert' or wilderness … a reminder to us that when we feel that we are in a desert place in our lives, we should not give up hope. It may be that God's grace will come to us at any moment. Have you had an experience of God's grace coming to you when you were in a desert place?

c) John calls the people to repentance (= a change of heart), as a way to a new life. Can you recall times when you had a change of heart, and the change led to new life for you?

d) John baptised people with water as a gesture to mark their change of heart. Sometimes we perform an action to symbolise our change of heart – write a letter, throw away our last cigarettes etc. Can you remember a symbolic gesture with which you marked a change of heart?

e) John did not claim to be greater than he was and freely acknowledged the greater role that Jesus would play. When have you seen yourself, or others, act with that kind of humility, freely acknowledging the place of God and of others in what is happening? What difference does it make to you when you are comfortable with your own important, but limited, worth?

Prayer

With tender comfort and transforming power you come into our midst, O God of mercy and might. Make ready a way in the wilderness, clear a straight path in our hearts, and form us into a repentant people, that the advent of your Son may find us watchful and eager for the glory he reveals. We ask this through him whose coming is certain, whose day draws near: your Son, our Lord Jesus Christ, who lives and reigns with you in the unity of the Holy Spirit, God for ever and ever. Amen.

🌿 Second Reading 🌿

2 Pet 3:8 But do not ignore this one fact, beloved, that with the Lord one day is like a thousand years, and a thousand years are like one day. [9] The Lord is not slow about his promise, as some think of slowness, but is patient with you, not wanting any to perish, but all to come to repentance. [10] But the day of the Lord will come like a thief, and then the heavens will pass away with a loud noise, and the elements will be dissolved with fire, and the earth and everything that is done on it will be disclosed.

[11] Since all these things are to be dissolved in this way, what sort of persons ought you to be in leading lives of holiness and godliness, [12] waiting for and hastening the coming of the day of God, because of which the heavens will be set ablaze and dissolved, and the elements will melt with fire? [13] But, in accordance with his promise, we wait for new heavens and a new earth, where righteousness is at home.

[14] Therefore, beloved, while you are waiting for these things, strive to be found by him at peace, without spot or blemish; [15] *and regard the patience of our Lord as salvation. So also our beloved brother Paul wrote to you according to the wisdom given him,* [16] *speaking of this as he does in all his letters. There are some things in them hard to understand, which the ignorant and unstable twist to their own destruction, as they do the other scriptures.*

Initial observations

The reading fits in with the other readings for the second Sunday of Advent and it can be read in a straightforward way for its exhortation. At the same time, it must be confessed that the apocalyptic imagery, always colourful, is something of a block today. A contextualised reading, however, should permit a richer interpretation.

Kind of writing

2 Peter combines two kinds of writing, the letter and the testament. By the time it was written, the letter had become the standard format for Christian instruction (as a glance at a New Testament shows). However, within that format we also find testamentary passages.

The question of its relationship to Jude is enlivened by the great number of parallels between these two documents. Because of its references, it looks as if it was written after the collection and circulation of Paul's letters (see the added v. 15), and after 1 Peter and Jude. Some scholars point to a date as late as 120–150 for the approximate time of writing.

As for the context, the opponents seem to be an extreme evolution/distortion of Paul's doctrine of grace. This has led to licentiousness (cf. 1 Corinthians 6:12; 10:23) on the moral level, and a complete abandonment of eschatology on the spiritual level. The tension between the 'already' and the 'not yet' has been decided comprehensively in favour of the former. Hence, the insistence on understanding the delay of the Second Coming in the passage selected in the lectionary.

    1:1–2 Greeting
    1:3–11 God's blessing
    1:12–3:16 Testament
    3:17–18a: Closing exhortation
    3:18b Doxology
    The testament itself:
    1:12–15 A personal reflection
    1:16–21 Insistence
    2:1–22 Attacking false teachers
    3:1–16 The Second Coming

It would be good to read all of chapter 3.

Origin of the reading

The context of writing cannot be separated from the question of authorship. Almost unanimously, critical scholars regard 2 Peter as one of the very latest New Testament documents, written in the *name* of Peter and perhaps even in some Petrine tradition, but not actually by the apostle.

Related passages

> For a thousand years in your sight are like yesterday when it is past, or like a watch in the night. (Psalms 90:4)

> Have I any pleasure in the death of the wicked, says the Lord God, and not rather that they should turn from their ways and live? (Ezekiel 18:23)

> Then the Lord said, 'You are concerned about the bush, for which you did not labour and which you did not grow; it came into being in a night and perished in a night. And should I not be concerned about Nineveh, that great city, in which there are more than a hundred and twenty thousand persons who do not know their right hand from their left, and also many animals?' (Jonah 4:10–11)

Brief commentary

(V. 8)
This is the one thing which the false teachers ignore. They ignore God's word (see vv. 5–7), God's time (v. 8) and the patience of God (vv. 9 and 15).

(V. 9)
Many passages of scripture are alluded to (see above).

(V. 10)
See similar expressions in Matthew 24:43; Luke 19:36; 1 Thessalonians 5:2, 4; Revelation 3:3; 16:15.

(Vv. 11–12)
The language reflects the outlook of apocalyptic and, at the same time, the early Pauline metaphor of a new creation (2 Corinthians 5:17; Galatians 6:15). Apocalypse means literally revelation, and apocalypses of the period (include the book of Revelation) offer not so much *descriptions* of the end but rather *affirmations* that there is a saving purpose, that God shows himself to be faithful and that there will be a time of judgment. What will happen *then* is meant to trigger a different question: how should we act *now*?

(V. 13)

Believers are to match God's patience with their own. Good moral living will bring forward the end. As always in Jewish apocalyptic, God's final faithfulness is affirmed.

(v. 14)

It is not that the day will *never* come; rather in the meantime how should we live? For spot or blemish, see Ephesians 1:4; Colossians 1:22; 1 Thessalonians 3:13. To be 'found' is positive in the New Testament. For the suddenness of salvation, see Matthew 23:43–44; 1 Thessalonians 5:12; Revelation 3:3. It might be better to translate 'by him', which suggests agency, with the simpler 'in his presence'.

Pointers for prayer

a) As Christians even today we live between the 'already' and the 'not yet', sure of God's presence and yet hoping and yearning for its fulfilment. Can you identify with this in your own life?

b) Words like holiness and godliness seem to come from another time and yet conversion is never 'done'. How do I see my faith evolving over the next few years?

c) It is possible to be money rich and time poor, in the contemporary idiom. What is your experience of the quality and use of time in your life? Can we regard time as a gift of the Lord's patience, as he waits for us to continue on the path of true discipleship?

Prayer

Timeless God, we come to you through your gift of time, fleeting and yet real and grace filled. Help us to use the time we have well and to recognise the times of your coming to us, that we may be ready with open hearts to receive you. We make our prayer through Christ our Lord. Amen.

🍃 First Reading 🍃

Is 40:1 Comfort, O comfort my people, says your God. ² Speak tenderly to Jerusalem, and cry to her that she has served her term, that her penalty is paid, that she has received from the LORD's hand double for all her sins.

[3] A voice cries out: 'In the wilderness prepare the way of the LORD, make straight in the desert a highway for our God. [4] Every valley shall be lifted up, and every mountain and hill be made low; the uneven ground shall become level, and the rough places a plain. [5] Then the glory of the LORD shall be revealed, and all people shall see it together, for the mouth of the LORD has spoken.'

[9] Get you up to a high mountain, O Zion, herald of good tidings; lift up your voice with strength, O Jerusalem, herald of good tidings, lift it up, do not fear; say to the cities of Judah, 'Here is your God!' [10] See, the Lord GOD comes with might, and his arm rules for him; his reward is with him, and his recompense before him. [11] He will feed his flock like a shepherd; he will gather the lambs in his arms, and carry them in his bosom, and gently lead the mother sheep.

Initial observations

To use a modern cliché, this is the iconic reading for Advent. It is, of course, a wonderful reading, full of hope and vision, as familiar to us from the opening of Handel's *Messiah*, as from the Bible itself. V. 3 is used in Mark's Gospel to introduce and 'locate' John the Baptist.

Kind of writing

This passage is a very fine example of biblical poetry. Almost every two lines illustrate poetic parallelism. You might notice that the second line is not simply a repetition in other words but actually brings forward the thought. Robert Alter speaks of the 'uneasy synonymity' of biblical poetry. For example:

... that she has served her term, that her penalty is paid, that she has received from the Lord's hand double for all her sins.

Three systems of metaphors are intertwined: forensic (sin and punishment, reward and recompense), construction (roads and highways, hills and mountains), pastoral (shepherding). The language of shepherding echoes at the end the words of compassion and tenderness at the start.

Origin of the reading

As noted regularly, the book of Isaiah seems to have been produced in three distinct phases. Our reading today opens the section (chs 40–55) proclaimed and written down during the Babylonian Exile (587–539 BC). That exile was experienced and remembered as the greatest calamity to fall upon the people of Israel.

The tragedy triggered an intense questioning and eventually a prodigious renewal of faith at all levels. So much is this the case that it may be said the exiles went out *Israelites* and came back *Jews*. This is not only because only one of the twelve tribes seems to have survived – the Judeans/the Jews – but because in Exile they took up the distinctive marks of Judaism as we know it up to today. These include the dietary laws, Sabbath observance, perhaps moving circumcision from puberty to birth and, eventually, even the synagogue.

Related passages

Shepherding language is found widely, starting with the call of David (1 Samuel 16:6–13) and, famously, in Psalm 23, *The Lord is my shepherd*. Ezekiel 34 is especially intense, as a few verses will illustrate.

> I myself will be the shepherd of my sheep, and I will make them lie down, says the Lord GOD. I will seek the lost, and I will bring back the strayed, and I will bind up the injured, and I will strengthen the weak, but the fat and the strong I will destroy. I will feed them with justice. (Ezekiel 34:15–16)

Brief commentary

(V. 1)
'My people' and 'your God' are measures of intimacy. The repetition of comfort is insistent.

(V. 2)

Behind the forensic imagery lies the discernment that the Exile was a kind of punishment or at least had to be treated as an opportunity for purification.

(V. 3)

Whose voice? The herald who will bring the news to Zion. Notice it is not a highway *to* our God but *for* our God. This implies God returns with the exiles and, consequently, God was with them all along, even if they were not aware of him.

(V. 4)

The topography (used in metaphor) really does reflect the return from Babylon but echoes the Exodus from Egypt. The prophet portrays the return as a new Exodus, now that the liberator God has acted once more.

(V. 5)

God's glory is God's identity as saving presence. The root meaning of 'glory' in Hebrew is weight or heaviness. This easily shifted to mean reputation and honour. Still, glory as substantial presence rather than external appearance is in view.

(V. 9)

The herald is to speak from places significant in Jewish memory: Zion and Jerusalem.

(V. 10)

God's arm symbolises God's power – but exercised, as we see in the next verse, like a shepherd.

(V. 11)

A great biblical theme – God as shepherd of his people – is used again to give new hope to those in Exile. It is a detailed, very tender description.

Pointers for prayer

a) Can I remember difficult experiences in my life, which in retrospect turned out to be moments of grace? What about my life and challenges at present?

d) In the life of prayer, it often seems God is absent, especially in difficult times. How do I become aware of this hidden presence of God?

e) Often there are 'things' in my life which make it difficult for me to open my whole self to God. What are my mountains and valleys? How do I make a straight highway for my God?

f) A great and constant message in the Bible is encapsulated in two phrases: 'Do not fear' and 'Here is your God'. We all need that deep reassurance.

g) We are carried through life by others, by their love and concern, and by God who comes to those 'who know their need of God', the poor in spirit. Acknowledgement of the times God has borne me through shadows and dark valleys.

Prayer

God of love, speak to us your word of comfort that we may be encouraged to lift our voices and acknowledge, 'Here is our God.'
As you have cared for us like a shepherd, may we too care for all among whom we live, that your Gospel
may not only be heard in words but also seen in deeds.
We make our prayer through Christ our Lord. Amen.

Themes across the readings

The citation in Mark 1:2–3, attributed to Isaiah alone, actually comes from two passages, Malachi 3:1 and Isaiah 40:3, as we saw. The link is an expectation that a prophet like Elijah would introduce the Messiah to Israel. But there is more. The Isaiah reading resembles the first notes of an overture – something new and grand is coming to be, echoing the Exodus itself. In the opening of the Jesus story, something not just new or revolutionary is taking place but rather something utterly without parallel: Jesus the Christ, the Son of God, is coming among us.

Chapter 3

Advent 3B

Thought for the day

In the words of John's Gospel, John the Baptist came as a witness, to speak for the light, the true light who was coming into the world. In this season of Advent, the Baptist points us towards the coming one and he invites us to reflect on our need of the light of Jesus in the darkness of our lives. Darkness means many things: a sense of being lost, a lack of direction, helplessness, sin or, indeed, lack of faith. This Christmas, may the God who said, 'Let light shine out of darkness', 'shine in our hearts to give the light of the knowledge of the glory of God in the face of Jesus Christ' (2 Corinthians 4:6).

Prayer

We come before you in the darkness of our lives, aware of our need of Christ, the light of the world. Let us receive him in faith so that we may become witnesses to that light which has truly come into the world. We make this prayer through Christ our Lord. Amen.

🌿 Gospel 🌿

Jn 1:6 There was a man sent from God, whose name was John. ⁷ He came as a witness to testify to the light, so that all might believe through him. ⁸ He himself was not the light, but he came to testify to the light.

Jn 1:19 This is the testimony given by John when the Jews sent priests and Levites from Jerusalem to ask him, 'Who are you?' [20] He confessed and did not deny it, but confessed, 'I am not the Messiah.' [21] And they asked him, 'What then? Are you Elijah?' He said, 'I am not.' 'Are you the prophet?' He answered, 'No.' [22] Then they said to him, 'Who are you? Let us have an answer for those who sent us. What do you say about yourself?' [23] He said, 'I am the voice of one crying out in the wilderness, "Make straight the way of the Lord," as the prophet Isaiah said'.

[24] Now they had been sent from the Pharisees. [25] They asked him, 'Why then are you baptising if you are neither the Messiah, nor Elijah, nor the prophet?' [26] John answered them, 'I baptise with water. Among you stands one whom you do not know, [27] the one who is coming after me; I am not worthy to untie the thong of his sandal.' [28] This took place in Bethany across the Jordan where John was baptising.

Initial observations

The community of the Fourth Gospel came from different backgrounds: followers of John the Baptist, Pharisees, Samaritans and Gentiles. Because of the continuing existence of disciples of John, the anxiety vis–à–vis the Baptist is even more heightened here than elsewhere.

Four examples may suffice: the poetry of the Prologue is interrupted by prose (today's first paragraph), designed to put John in the second division; John is then made *himself* to quote the Old Testament citation at the start of Mark's account; the baptism of Jesus by John is not recounted, although associated phenomena are; the death of John is not presented in order to prevent any comparisons with the unique 'lifting up' of the Son of Man.

Kind of writing

There are three moments in the text.
(i) Vv. 6–8 are prose commentary by the writer on the identity of John.

(ii) Vv. 19–23 constitute technically a *chreia*, that is an anecdote or scene with a point, developed in the form of questions and answers and ending conclusively with a citation of God's word from the prophet Isaiah.

(iii) Vv. 24–28 go back to the theme of comparison and make explicit the distinction between John and Jesus.

Old Testament background

There is clear reference to the first reading of last Sunday's Mass:

> A voice cries out: 'In the wilderness prepare the way of the LORD, make straight in the desert a highway for our God.' (Isaiah 40:3) As in Mark's version, this text is adjusted to read as follows: A voice cried out in the wilderness: 'Prepare the way of the Lord.' The shift in punctuation mirrors the new application to the Baptist. From a practical point of view, a voice crying out the wilderness would not have made a lot of sense.

New Testament foreground

Mark implies that John was Elijah and Matthew makes it explicit. In this gospel, however, John himself *denies* he was the anticipated Elijah figure. Furthermore, in this gospel there is a nuanced appreciation of who he was: the voice in relation to the word, the best man ('the friend') in relation to the bridegroom.

'He who has the *bride* is the *bridegroom*. The *friend of the bridegroom*, who stands and hears him, rejoices greatly at the *bridegroom's* voice. For this reason my joy has been fulfilled' (John 3:29).

At this point in John 3, it is apparently the Baptist who is speaking. The picture of John the Baptist in the Gospel of John is very clearly focused, and it may be summed up in one of the gospel's pungent statements: 'He was not the light, but came to bear witness to the light' (1:8).

St Paul

Besides this, you know what time it is, how it is now the moment for you to wake from sleep. For salvation is nearer to us now than when we became believers; the night is far gone, the day is near. Let us then lay aside the works of darkness and put on the armour of light; let us live honourably as in the day, not in revelling and drunkenness, not in debauchery and licentiousness, not in quarrelling and jealousy. Instead, put on the Lord Jesus Christ, and make no provision for the flesh, to gratify its desires. (Romans 13:11–14) Cf. 1 Thessalonians 4:15–5:11.

Brief commentary

(V. 6)
The first statement is positive: John was sent by God. 'Send' is an important word in the Fourth Gospel, being almost a name for God who sends Jesus, John and, eventually, Jesus' disciples.

(V. 7)
Witness is also a key category in the gospel: John 1:7; 3:28; 8:17.

(V. 8)
Naturally, it is Jesus himself who is the light. 'Again Jesus spoke to them, saying, "I am the light of the world. Whoever follows me will never walk in darkness but will have the light of life"' (John 8:12). 'As long as I am in the world, I am the light of the world' (John 9:5). 'I have come as light into the world, so that everyone who believes in me should not remain in the darkness' (John 12:46).

(V. 19)
This is a real question, already asked by Jesus in the Synoptic Gospels: 'Did the baptism of John come from heaven, or was it of human origin? Answer me' (Mark 11:30).

(V. 20)
Notice the triple insistence: he confessed, did not deny, confessed. The expectation of a Messiah as such is not attested in the Hebrew Bible but it is in the later non–biblical books of Judaism, such as the Dead Sea Scrolls or the Psalms of Solomon. It is not without significance that the first things John says are denials of mistaken identity. Lest there should be any lack of clarity, the writer makes him repeat the denial later in the story: 'You yourselves are my witnesses that I said, "I am not the Messiah, but I have been sent ahead of him"' (John 3:28).

(V. 21)

There was an expectation that Elijah would be part of the final unfolding, based on Malachi 4:5. Likewise, there was an expectation that a prophet like Moses would be part of the end, based on Deuteronomy 18:15.

(V. 22)

After all the denials, this is a good question.

(V. 23)

Here the author plays his trump card – he makes *John himself* cite the Isaiah text, which allocates to him a preparatory role and nothing more.

(V. 24)

All religions use water symbolism and Judaism is no exception. However, the once-off baptism of John was exceptional and required interpretation. The questioners also summarise the denials, a technique of emphasis and insistence.

(V. 25)

John uses the opportunity not to explain his baptism but to point to Jesus. We expect a line such as 'but he will baptism with the Spirit' but instead we are offered 'whom you do *not* know', a resonant theme in this gospel.

(V. 26–27)

An explicit echo of the synoptic traditions: 'He proclaimed, 'The one who is more powerful than I is coming after me; I am not worthy to stoop down and untie the thong of his sandals' (Mark 1:7; see also Luke 3:16; Acts 13:25).

(V. 28)

In this gospel, *Jesus* is also shown baptising: 'After this Jesus and his disciples went into the Judean countryside, and he spent some time there with them and baptised. John also was baptising at Aenon near Salim because water was abundant there; and people kept coming and were being baptised' (John 3:22–23; see also John 3:26; 4:1–2; 10:40). In chapter 4 it says Jesus did *not* baptise.

Pointers for prayer

a) John the Baptist came to bear witness to Jesus. Who have been the people who have borne witness to you of the good news of the gospel that God loves you – a friend, a parent, a teacher, for example? To whom have you borne that witness?

b) John appears in the story as one who had the courage to be himself in the face of loud and aggressive people. He was also a person who knew his own value, did not make exaggerated claims and was content with his mission. Can you recall times when you have been able to be yourself, even in the face of criticism from others?

c) John was 'the voice of one crying out in the wilderness' – announcing confidently to those in the wilderness that they must not despair because God's grace will come to them at any moment. Have you had the experience of being in the wilderness, feeling lost? From whom did you hear a voice that gave you hope? Have you been able to give hope to other people when they were in the wilderness?

d) The priests and Levites challenged John the Baptist on his authority for speaking as he did and tried to put a label on him so that they could more easily dismiss what he had to say. When were you open to accepting a truth from a person whom you had previously dismissed as having nothing to say to you?

Prayer

O God, most high and most near, you send glad tidings to the lowly, you hide not your face from the poor; those who dwell in darkness you call into the light.

Take away our blindness, remove the hardness of our hearts, and form us into a humble people, that, at the advent of your Son, we may recognise him in our midst and find joy in his saving presence.

This prayer we make through him whose coming is certain, whose day draws near, your Son, Jesus Christ, who lives and reigns with you, in the unity of the Holy Spirit, God, for ever and ever. Amen.

🌿 Second Reading 🌿

1 Thess 5:12 *Now we ask you, brothers and sisters, to acknowledge those who labour among you and preside over you in the Lord and admonish you,* [13] *and to esteem them most highly in love because of their work. Be at peace among yourselves.* [14] *And we urge you, brothers and sisters, admonish the undisciplined, comfort the discouraged, help the weak, be patient towards all.* [15] *See that no one pays back evil for evil to anyone, but always pursue what is good for one another and for all.* [16] Always rejoice, [17] constantly pray, [18] in everything give thanks. For this is God's will for you in Christ Jesus. [19] Do not extinguish the Spirit. [20] Do not treat prophecies with contempt. [21] But examine all things; hold fast to what is good. [22] Stay away from every form of evil. [23] Now may the God of peace himself make you completely holy and may your spirit and soul and body be kept entirely blameless at the coming of our Lord Jesus Christ. [24] He who calls you is trustworthy, and he will in fact do this.

Initial observations

The joy of the Gospel is very evident in the writings of St Paul (see more texts below). This is true also in Paul's very first letter, 1 Thessalonians. Joy is emphasised even though believers may have been undergoing tremendous challenges. In 2 Corinthians he refers again to the Christians in Macedonia (of which Thessalonica was the Roman capital): *We want you to know, brothers and sisters, about the grace of God that has been granted to the churches of Macedonia; for during a severe ordeal of affliction, their abundant joy and their extreme poverty have overflowed in a wealth of generosity on their part* (2 Corinthians 8:1–2).

Kind of writing

The whole of 1 Thessalonians is a letter laid out using the structure of a speech. Thus, it may be read in two tenses, epistolary and rhetorical.
1:1 Letter superscript
    1:2–10 Thanksgiving / *introduction*

1:9–10 Topic, in three parts
2:1–3:12 *Relationships*
4:1–12 *Holiness*
4:13–5:11 *End time issues*
5:12–23 Exhortation/*conclusion*
5:24 Letter postscript

Our reading, accordingly, comes from the second half of the closing exhortation and the final postscript. It happens in Paul's letters that at the final words of encouragement, he falls into a kind of *staccato* writing, with a pile-up of pithy imperatives. See Romans 12:9–14 below.

Origin of the reading

Writing probably from Corinth, Paul needed to rebuild relationships with the Christians in Thessalonica. They also had questions to which he responded in the letter: What happens to the dead? When will the end be? Paul had spent enough time in their city to establish a community with leaders, who are mentioned in the slightly expanded reading above.

Related passages

Love must be without hypocrisy. Abhor what is evil, cling to what is good. Be devoted to one another with mutual love, showing eagerness in honouring one another. Do not lag in zeal, be enthusiastic in spirit, serve the Lord. *Rejoice* in hope, endure in suffering, persist in prayer. Contribute to the needs of the saints, pursue hospitality. Bless those who persecute you, bless and do not curse. (Romans 12:9–14)

Rejoice in the Lord always. Again I say, *rejoice*! Let everyone see your gentleness. The Lord is near! Do not be anxious about anything. Instead, in every situation, through prayer and petition with thanksgiving, tell your requests to God. And the peace of God that surpasses all understanding will guard your hearts and minds in Christ Jesus (Philippians 4:4–7).

Brief commentary

(V. 16)

Joy does not exclude suffering; on the contrary, they often go together. For joy, both as verb and noun, as a feature of Paul's worldview, see: Romans 12:12, 15; 14:17; 15:13, 32; 16:19; 1 Corinthians 7:30; 13:6; 16:17; 2 Corinthians 1:24; 2:3; 6:10; 7:4, 7, 9, 13, 16; 8:2; 13:9, 11; Galatians 5:22; Philippians 1:4, 18, 25; 2:2, 17–18, 28–29; 3:1; 4:1, 4, 10; 1 Thessalonians 1:6; 2:19–20; 3:9; 5:16; Philemon 1:7. As you can see, all seven uncontested letters are represented.

(Vv. 17–18)

Paul himself is a man of constant prayer, as a glance at the thanksgivings which open six of the uncontested letters (Galatians has none) will show.

(Vv. 19–20)

There is no hint that they were *quenching* the Spirit (see 1 Thessalonians 1:5–7). V. 20 is the only mention in this letter of Christian prophecy, important elsewhere for Paul (1 Corinthians 14).

(Vv. 21–22)

These instructions are useful at any time and here are examples of the *staccato* imperatives.

(V. 23)

Like many a preacher, Paul frequently concludes his persuasion with a prayer, not only drawing the various threads together but also bringing the hearers consciously into God's presence. In particular, there is an emphatic echo of the thanksgiving at the start of the letter (1:2–10).

(V. 24)

The emphasis on the faithfulness of God may seem redundant to us. However, it is very rooted in the Old Testament (e.g. Deuteronomy 7:9, 32:4 and many others) and it was also part of the apocalyptic worldview. That worldview asked where was God in the midst of persecution and death, and the answer is always 'God is faithful'. In Jewish tradition, God's faithfulness will be evident in the resurrection of the dead. In

Christian tradition, God's faithfulness is also apparent in Jesus' crucifixion (see Romans 3:21–26 in the NET translation). A faithful God was also a contrast with the fickle arbitrariness of the (frequently immoral) deities of Greece and Rome. Cf. *You turned to God from idols, to serve a living and true God* (1 Thessalonians 1:9).

Pointers for prayer

a) If someone were to describe my experience of 'the joy of the Gospel', where would I begin? Has it been my experience that joy and suffering can go together?

b) For what should I give thanks to God at this point in my life? According to Meister Eckhardt, if the only prayer we ever said was one of thanksgiving it would be sufficient.

c) God is faithful. Can I name my own experience of God's faithfulness to me?

Prayer

Living and faithful God, in you we find the deep springs of love and joy.
Help us to embrace these gifts that others may be drawn
to the Good News in Jesus.

Grant this through him, your Son, our Lord Jesus Christ, who lives and reigns with you in the unity of the Holy Spirit, God for ever and ever.
Amen.

🌿 First Reading 🌿

Is 61:1 The spirit of the Lord God is upon me, because the Lord has anointed me; he has sent me to bring good news to the oppressed, to bind up the brokenhearted, to proclaim liberty to the captives, and release to the prisoners; ² to proclaim the year of the Lord's favour, and the day of vengeance of our God; to comfort all who mourn;

Is 61:10 I will greatly rejoice in the Lord, my whole being shall exult in my God; for he has clothed me with the garments of salvation, he has covered me with the robe of righteousness, as a bridegroom decks himself with a garland, and as a bride adorns herself with her jewels. [11] For as the earth brings forth its shoots, and as a garden causes what is sown in it to spring up, so the Lord GOD will cause righteousness and praise to spring up before all the nations.

Initial observations

Only four verses, but how deep and rich! It would be hard not to be moved by the hope and energy of these lines.

Kind of writing

In times of plenty and apparent stability, the prophets warn and threaten. In times when unending disaster seems all there is, they speak words of life, energy and joy. This is not just because they are members of the awkward squad. Prophets shake people out of slumber and complacency to take hold again of the reality of God and the truly endless potential of life with God on our side.

Origin of the reading

The reading comes from a long poem in Third Isaiah (Isaiah 61) of which we read the first two and the last two verses.

Related passages

(1) *Spirit anointing*
Here is my servant, whom I uphold, my chosen, in whom my soul delights; I have put my spirit upon him; he will bring forth justice to the nations. He will not cry or lift up his voice, or make it heard in the street; a bruised reed he will not break, and a dimly burning wick he will not quench; he will faithfully bring forth justice. He will not grow faint or be crushed until he has established justice in the earth; and the coastlands wait for his teaching. (Isaiah 42:1–4)

(2) *Marriage metaphors*

In the heavens he has set a tent for the sun, which comes out like a bridegroom from his wedding canopy, and like a strong man runs its course with joy. Its rising is from the end of the heavens, and its circuit to the end of them; and nothing is hid from its heat. (Psalm 19:4–6)

You shall no more be termed Forsaken, and your land shall no more be termed Desolate; but you shall be called My Delight Is in Her, and your land Married; for the LORD delights in you, and your land shall be married. For as a young man marries a young woman, so shall your builder marry you, and as the bridegroom rejoices over the bride, so shall your God rejoice over you. (Isaiah 62:4–5)

(3) *Jubilee year*

And you shall hallow the fiftieth year and you shall proclaim liberty throughout the land to all its inhabitants. It shall be a jubilee for you: you shall return, every one of you, to your property and every one of you to your family. That fiftieth year shall be a jubilee for you: you shall not sow, or reap the after-growth, or harvest the unpruned vines. For it is a jubilee; it shall be holy to you: you shall eat only what the field itself produces. (Leviticus 25:10–12)

Brief commentary

(V. 1)

This is an evocation of Isaiah 42:1–9 and 49:1–6. Anointed gives us the word *messiah*, literally anointed one. The verses list conditions of oppression (broken-hearted, captives, prisoners) and the good news of God (to bind up, liberty, release).

(V. 2)

The Year of Jubilee, at least in theory, was a year of rest for the land and, in a way, rest for the people, a kind of sabbatical *avant le mot*. So that people would not be trapped forever in cycles of never-ending indebtedness, it was also to be a time when all loans were remitted.

Vengeance here does not mean vendetta, it means rather God's energy for what is right and just. The mourners are not simply the bereaved; it also means those who are not afraid to recognise and name the present difficulties. Not accidentally, the Exile came to an end after some fifty years of servitude – it was time for rest and jubilation.

(V. 10)

At the end of the poem, a note of intense joy is struck. These two verses are really a thanksgiving song. The language moves from internal feeling to outward expression and from there to comparison with a wedding. Salvation and justice (righteousness) are really the one thing and God's love is also God's acting justly to all. Earlier in Isaiah 59:15–17 and later in 63:1–9, God fighting for justice will wear garments of vengeance and robes soaked in blood. The contrast is all the greater, when we see what kind of garments the faithful will wear.

(V. 11)

Continuing the note of joy, a spring garden is painted before our eyes. It is not only a metaphor. God causes the garden to grow miraculously. He can also act on humans so as to bring about endless praise. Even the nations will see, eventually, God's justice towards and vindication of the faithfulness of Israel.

Pointers for prayer

a) All disciples, without distinction, have a calling from God, God who has anointed each of us to bear the Good News. How do I live and make real this responsibility for the Gospel in our day?

b) Perhaps I can identify or could identify in the past with the oppressed and the broken-hearted, the captives and the prisoners. What gives me sustenance? How have I experienced and lived 'being set free'?

c) On this third Sunday of Advent our them is joy, really anticipatory joy as we approach the feast of Christ's birth. Joy, while not always overt, is part and parcel of being Christian.

d) Perhaps I have a garden and know from first-hand experience

the wonder of planting and seeing my own flowers and vege-
tables grow. Brown earth becomes a tulip, beautiful to look at,
or an apple, delicious to eat. The same creator God is at work
in me, causing 'righteousness and praise' to spring up in and
through all who believe in him.

Prayer

Creator God, you know our needs better than we do ourselves.
Send into our hearts your Spirit of life and love that we may know the joy
of your presence in our lives. Open in us the springs of joy and praise that
our whole life may witness to you, creator and giver of all.
We make our prayer through Christ our Lord. Amen.

Themes across the readings

There is an anticipation of the gospel in the first reading, in so far as the
prologue of John (1:6–8) speaks of the light that is Christ. But the real
link is with the second reading today. Both the prophet and Paul take up
the theme of rejoicing, on this third Sunday of Advent, and both speak
of the Spirit to be given. God's very own faithfulness – to himself and
to his people – is the foundation of Christian faith and hope and joy.
Exceptionally, the responsorial 'psalm' is not a psalm at all, but a canti-
cle from the New Testament. This prayer is well chosen as part of the
lead-up to the Christmas celebration. It expresses a kind of bubbling,
uncontainable joy in God's presence. At the same time, it does not omit
the concerns of justice, as we hear in Luke 1:52–55.

Chapter 4

Advent 4B

Thought for the day

The season of preparation is drawing to a close. Like Mary, our getting ready involves deep listening to what God is asking of me now and an interior willingness to say 'let what you have said be done to me.' What is God asking of me now, as a person, in the family, at work, and indeed within the faith community of the Church? Have I noticed a pattern of 'nudges' from God calling me to a deeper, perhaps different engagement as a disciple? Are my gifts – tokens of God's grace – fully at the service of my neighbour?

Prayer

Great and loving God, open my ear to your word, open my heart to your call, open my life to your service. Give us all the strength to live according to the Good News of your Son, Jesus, our Lord. Amen.

Gospel

Lk 1:26 In the sixth month the angel Gabriel was sent by God to a town in Galilee called Nazareth, ²⁷ to a virgin engaged to a man whose name was Joseph, of the house of David. The virgin's name was Mary. ²⁸ And he came to her and said, 'Greetings, favoured one! The Lord is with you.' ²⁹ But she was much perplexed by his words and pondered what sort of greeting this might be. ³⁰ The angel said to her, 'Do not be afraid, Mary, for you have found favour with God. ³¹ And now, you will conceive in your womb and bear a son, and you will name him Jesus. [32] He will be great, and will be called the Son of the Most High, and the Lord God will give to him the throne of his ancestor David. [33] He will reign over the house of Jacob for ever, and of his kingdom there will be no end.'

[34] Mary said to the angel, 'How can this be, since I am a virgin?' [35] The angel said to her, 'The Holy Spirit will come upon you, and the power of the Most High will overshadow you; therefore the child to be born will be holy; he will be called Son of God. [36] And now, your relative Elizabeth in her old age has also conceived a son; and this is the sixth month for her who was said to be barren. [37] For nothing will be impossible with God.' [38] Then Mary said, 'Here am I, the servant of the Lord; let it be with me according to your word.' Then the angel departed from her.

Initial observations

The Annunciation to Mary is unique to Luke's Gospel. Three of the gospels enjoy an extended prologue: Luke 1–2, Matthew 1–2 and John 1. All three are explorations of the identity of Jesus before the Gospel narrative proper begins. The exploration is always in dialogue with Old Testament patterns and precedents.

Kind of writing

Annunciation
An annunciation type-scene follows a predictable pattern. The basic pattern is well recognised:
1. Appearance of an angel
2. Fear/prostration
3. Reassurance
4. Message
5. Objection
6. Sign

The Future Accomplishments of the Child

2 Samuel 7:9, 13–14, 16. Cf. also Psalms 2:7 and 89:29; Isaiah 9:5-6; 11:1-2; 2 Samuel 7:14

The Portrait of Mary

Compare Mark 3:20–21 with Luke 11:14–16; and Mark 3:31–35 with Luke 8:19–21. Compare Mark 6:4 with Luke 4:24. Mary is a figure of faith after the model of Abraham.

Old Testament background

First of all, the story belongs to a type of story familiar from elsewhere in the Bible – Ishmael, Isaac, Samson, John the Baptist and even Jesus again in Matthew are all born as a result of a special intervention from on high. The pattern of these tales is noticed below. Whenever you have a pattern like this, the thing to look out for is how the pattern is being used in this concrete instance – where is it predictable and familiar? Where is it new and different?

New Testament foreground

We explore within Luke–Acts echoes of themes enunciated here. The abundance of cross references – verging on the pedantic – serves to makes the point.

The *joy of salvation* is a large theme in Luke–Acts (Luke 1:14, 28; 2:10; 6:23; 8:13; 10:17, 20; 13:17; 15:5, 7, 10, 32; 19:6, 37; 22:5; 23:8; 24:41, 52; Acts 5:41; 8:8, 39; 11:23; 12:14; 13:48, 52; 15:3, 23, 31; 23:26).

Grace and being graced (Luke 1:28, 30; 2:40, 52; 4:22; 6:32–34; 17:9; Acts 2:47; 4:33; 6:8; 7:10, 46; 11:23; 13:43; 14:3, 26; 15:11, 40; 18:27; 20:24, 32; 24:27; 25:3, 9).

David is frequently evoked (Luke 1:27, 32, 69; 2:4, 11; 3:31; 6:3; 18:38–39; 20:41–42, 44; Acts 1:16; 2:25, 29, 34; 4:25; 7:45; 13:22, 34, 36; 15:16).

Jacob too is recalled in the Gospel and Acts (Luke 1:33; 3:34; 13:28; 20:37; Acts 3:13; 7:8, 12, 14–15, 32, 46).

Do not be afraid (Luke 1:13, 30; 2:10; 5:10; 8:50; 12:7, 32; Acts 18:9; 27:24).

The *Holy Spirit* has a vast presence in Luke–Acts (Luke 1:15, 35, 41, 67; 2:25–26; 3:16, 22; 4:1; 10:21; 11:13; 12:10, 12; Acts 1:2, 5, 8, 16; 2:4, 33, 38; 4:8, 25, 31; 5:3, 32; 6:5; 7:51, 55; 8:15, 17, 19; 9:17, 31; 10:38, 44–45, 47; 11:15–16, 24; 13:2, 4, 9, 52; 15:8, 28; 16:6; 19:2, 6; 20:23, 28; 21:11; 28:25).

Servant – male or female – is an important image across Luke–Acts (Luke 1:38, 48 [from the Magnificat]; 2:29; 7:2–3, 8, 10; 12:37, 43, 45–47; 14:17, 21–23; 15:22; 17:7, 9–10; 19:13, 15, 17, 22; 20:10–11; 22:50; Acts 2:18; 4:29; 16:17).

St Paul

From Paul, a slave of Christ Jesus, called to be an apostle, set apart for the gospel of God. This gospel he promised beforehand through his prophets in the holy scriptures, concerning his Son who was a descendant of David with reference to the flesh, who was appointed the Son-of-God-in-power according to the Holy Spirit by the resurrection from the dead, Jesus Christ our Lord. Through him we have received grace and our apostleship to bring about the obedience of faith among all the Gentiles on behalf of his name. You also are among them, called to belong to Jesus Christ. To all those loved by God in Rome, called to be saints: Grace and peace to you from God our Father and the Lord Jesus Christ! (Romans 1:1–7)

Brief commentary

(V. 26)
The sixth month is that of Elizabeth's pregnancy, as noted later. Gabriel describes himself earlier: *The angel replied, 'I am Gabriel. I stand in the presence of God, and I have been sent to speak to you and to bring you this good news'* (Luke 1:19). The *book of Jubilees* 16:12 (a non-canonical text) tells us that it was in the *sixth month* of the year that *Sarah* became pregnant.

(V. 27)

Virginity was considered an unfulfilled and unfortunate state. Joseph is a conscious echo of the Joseph of Genesis. It is important for early Christians that Jesus is of the house of David – this is found not only in the gospels but also in Paul (Romans 1:3). The name 'Mary' from the Hebrew Miriam means rebellion. This name has significance when you read the Magnificat politically.

(V. 28)

Literally, it would be a verb, 'graced'.

(V. 29)

This marks the second stage of the type-scene, that of fear and puzzlement.

(V. 30)

This is also a standard part of the formula. Many, many people in the Bible are told 'not to be afraid': Genesis 15:1; 21:17; 26:24; 35:17; 43:23; 46:3; 50:19; Exodus 14:13; 20:20; Numbers 21:34; Deuteronomy 7:18 etc. All of this echoes Isaiah 7:14.

(V. 31)

This echoes what was said of John the Baptist: *Your wife Elizabeth will bear you a son, and you will name him John.* (Luke 1:13).

(Vv. 32–33)

This is the message – the language is interesting: royal in three senses – sonship, descendant of David, kingdom. The early Christians were keen to express continuity with the Israelite/Jewish past, as a mark of God's continued faithfulness. The last line of v. 33 has found its way into the Creed.

(V. 34)

This is a strange objection, because we all know how babies are born. Objections elsewhere in these stories are advanced age and infertility. In a way, the birth of John the Baptist is really patterned on the Old Testament annunciations, while the birth of Jesus (here) is something extraordinarily new, signalled by the virginal conception.

(V. 35)

The Holy Spirit, who inaugurates the new age – in Pentecost, in Jesus' first sermon (Luke 4), and first of all in his birth. 'If you then, who are evil, know how to give good gifts to your children, how much more will the heavenly Father give the Holy Spirit to those who ask him!' (Luke 11:13).

(V. 36)

The proof is offered practically (Elizabeth) and theologically (God). Notice the joining of the two causes of Elizabeth's childlessness: too old and, in any case, not able to have children.

(V. 37)

The creator's actions are inscrutable. This echoes God's challenge in Genesis 18:14: Can anything said by God be impossible?

(V. 38)

On 'here I am', see Genesis 22:1; 46:2; Exodus 3:4; 1 Samuel 3:4–16; Psalm 40:7; Isaiah 6:8. At this point, Mary is the exemplary 'hearer of the word'.

Pointers for prayer

a) 'Greetings, favoured one. The Lord is with you'. We are all favoured ones and God is with us. Sometimes we are more aware of this than others. How have you experienced being a favoured person, one blessed by God? How have you experienced God's presence? Who has been Gabriel to you … a messenger of good news?

b) 'Do not be afraid.' Mary was perplexed by the words of the angel. Perhaps you too have sometimes been perplexed by life's path and wondered what it all meant. Perhaps at times you have doubted if God was really with you. In your troubled moments who has been an 'angel' helping to lower your anxiety?

c) The angel told Mary that it was through her fruitfulness that she would realise the truth of the greeting. New life would come into being through her, and it would be through the Spirit of God working in her. How and where have you experienced yourself as a source of life for others? Have you at times had the sense that the Spirit of God was at work in you?

d) Mary was taken by surprise by the invitation, but she did not tell the angel she was not ready, nor ask him to return later. She was prepared to go with the invitation even though it was not the 'right moment'. 'Here I am Lord.' What invitations have come to you at the 'wrong time' and how have you responded?

e) Mary's response serves as a model for us – as one saying 'yes' to what life offers. What is it like for you to say 'yes' to life? Perhaps at this moment in your life you are being invited to say 'Here I am, Lord'?

Prayer

Here in our midst, O God of mystery, you disclose the secret hidden for countless ages. For you we wait; for you we listen.

Upon hearing your voice may we, like Mary, embrace your will and become a dwelling fit for your Word.

We ask this through him whose coming is certain, whose day draws near: your Son, our Lord Jesus Christ, who lives and reigns with you in the unity of the Holy Spirit, God for ever and ever. Amen.

🌿 Second Reading 🌿

Rom 16:25 Now to him who is able to strengthen you according to my gospel and the proclamation of Jesus Christ, according to the revelation of the mystery that had been kept secret for long ages, 26 but now is disclosed, and through the prophetic scriptures has been made known to all the nations, according to the command of the eternal God, to bring about the obedience of faith – 27 to the only wise God, through Jesus Christ, be glory for ever! Amen. (NET)

Initial observations

The Jerusalem Bible (but not the Revised New Jerusalem Bible) sensibly makes three sentences of this elevated and dense passage. In the original, however, it is a single, somewhat awkward sentence, bringing Romans to a close on a synthetic note. However, it would appear that these verses do not come from the hand of the apostle himself but seem to be a later addition. Nevertheless, these verses summarise the whole letter.

Kind of writing

This is a doxology, a liturgical formula giving glory to God. These may be found elsewhere in the New Testament, especially in the Deutero-Pauline letters, and are typical of later Christian usage. The whole doxology is either lacking or located elsewhere (after 14:23 or 15:33) in other early manuscripts and most likely is not original to the letter. This does not mean it is not part of Scripture; it simply means that the boundary between text and tradition in antiquity was more fluid than we usually permit ourselves to imagine.

The present doxology may have entered the tradition in a special context. Marcion (c. AD 85–c.160). mutilated the letter to the Romans to fit his anti–Jewish opinions. As part of the Church response, later Paulinists inserted this doxology to counter Marcion. Traces of his supersessionism (the idea that Christianity *displaces* Judaism) are countered by the affirmation of continuity with the prophetic writings. See the editorial adjustments below.

Origin of the reading

The context of the Roman letter is clear enough. Paul wrote to the Romans *before* his final journey to Jerusalem to advise them on how to live together harmoniously. The presenting issue was conflict over how much of the Law should be observed / retained / set aside, with Christians of Jewish and Gentile extraction taking up opposing positions.

The context of the final doxology (our verses) seems to be different, reflecting a crisis triggered by Marcion, who radically separated the Old Testament from the New Testament, Judaism from Christianity. In pursuit of that, he reduced the emerging New Testament to ten letters of Paul (edited) and a version of the Gospel according to Luke (edited). He rejected the Jewish Scriptures entirely. This truly radical dichotomy between the Old and New Testaments was rejected as heretical (although such an impulse may still be felt at popular level).

Scholars have traced a potential Jewish form of the original, as follows, with later Christianising insertions in italics.

> **Rom 16:25** Now to him who is able to strengthen you *according to my gospel and the proclamation of Jesus Christ,* according to the revelation of the mystery that had been kept secret for long ages, [26] *but now is disclosed, and through the prophetic scriptures* has been made known *to all the nations,* according to the command of the eternal God, to bring about the obedience of faith – [27] to the only wise God, *through Jesus Christ,* be glory for ever! Amen.

Related passages

Examples of similar doxologies

> Now to him who by the power at work within us is able to accomplish abundantly far more than all we can ask or imagine, to him be glory in the Church and in Christ Jesus to all generations, forever and ever. Amen. (Ephesians 3:20–21)

> To the King of the ages, immortal, invisible, the only God, be honour and glory forever and ever. Amen. (1 Timothy 1:17)

> Now to him who is able to keep you from falling, and to make you stand without blemish in the presence of his glory with rejoicing, to the only God our Saviour, through Jesus Christ our Lord, be glory, majesty, power and authority, before all time and now and forever. Amen. (Jude 1:24–25)

> To him be the glory both now and to the day of eternity. Amen. (2 Peter 3:18)

Brief commentary

(V. 25)

Traces of genuine Pauline terminology are given a new context by the later language of orthodoxy (strengthen, revelation, mystery). 'According to the proclamation (*kerygma*) of Jesus Christ' is found nowhere else in the New Testament. Paul is thus yoked to later concerns.

(V. 26)

Again some genuinely Pauline terms are juxtaposed with the later language of emerging orthodoxy. At the later time, Christian *leaders* were referred to as prophets (Ephesians 2:20; 3:5; 4:11; Revelation 18:20; *Martyrdom of Polycarp* 16.2). 2 Peter 3:16 refers to Paul's letters as 'writings'. All the nations must include Jews as well, according to Romans 9–11 and the theme enunciated in Romans 1:16–17.

(V. 27)

God is wise because he has only now disclosed the secret of the mystery. The final phrase, literally 'from aeons to aeons', shifts the eschatological timeframe indeterminably.

Pointers for prayer

a) If you were to compose your own doxology, what would you include in your praise and thanksgiving to God?

b) The excitement of discovery is evident in these verses. When did you find yourself suddenly alive to the message of the Gospel? How are you today?

c) Living discipleship means attending to God's word and the promptings of the Spirit. Prayer: Lord, may your word penetrate my heart and change my life.

Prayer

God, we stand before the mystery of your being, in wonder and awe. You are greater than our hearts and yet we can love you in the Holy Spirit. You are greater than our minds, and yet we can know you in Jesus Christ.

Draw us every more deeply into your being that we come to that fulfilment which alone satisfies the longings of the human heart. Through Christ our Lord. Amen.

🌿 First Reading 🌿

2 Sam 7:1 Now when the king was settled in his house, and the LORD had given him rest from all his enemies around him, ² the king said to the prophet Nathan, 'See now, I am living in a house of cedar, but the ark of God stays in a tent.' ³ Nathan said to the king, 'Go, do all that you have in mind; for the LORD is with you.'

⁴ But that same night the word of the LORD came to Nathan: ⁵ Go and tell my servant David: Thus says the LORD: Are you the one to build me a house to live in?

2 Sam 7:8 Now therefore thus you shall say to my servant David: Thus says the LORD of hosts: I took you from the pasture, from following the sheep to be prince over my people Israel; ⁹ and I have been with you wherever you went, and have cut off all your enemies from before you; and I will make for you a great name, like the name of the great ones of the earth. ¹⁰ And I will appoint a place for my people Israel and will plant them, so that they may live in their own place, and be disturbed no more; and evildoers shall afflict them no more, as formerly, ¹¹ from the time that I appointed judges over my people Israel; and I will give you rest from all your enemies. Moreover the LORD declares to you that the LORD will make you a house.

2 Sam 7:16 Your house and your kingdom shall be made sure for ever before me; your throne shall be established for ever.

Initial observations

This reading is one of the key texts of the Hebrew Bible, for Jews first of all, but also for Christians. It forms the background to later hopes for a future David-like king and eventually the background for the early Christian identification of Jesus as a descendant of David (see Romans 1:3). It forms an appropriate passage to reflect upon as we approach the birth of 'David's son'. The full 2 Samuel 7 should be read to make sense of it all.

Kind of writing

The passage is full of royal ideology, but there is also a prophetic voice. Nathan has a very important role here, in 2 Samuel 12 and again in 1 Kings 1. Nathan makes David stop short of (literally!) domesticating God. At the same time, there is a powerful expression of God's own faithfulness.

Origin of the reading

The passage is a fairly straightforward narrative, taken from the second book of Samuel. There are really just two speeches, a short one by David and a much longer one by God. According to the text, David had just brought the ark of the covenant to Jerusalem, his capital. That was clearly a very political move. Before that, God's presence – symbolised by the ark – went with the people wherever they wandered, a kind of itinerant 'God of the open spaces' (one possible meaning of *El Shaddai*). By taking to himself the symbol of God's presence, David increased his power and control over people. Psalm 132 captures very much the same royal theology of the house of David.

Related passages

> As for you, if you will walk before me, as David your father walked, with integrity of heart and uprightness, doing according to all that I have commanded you, and keeping my statutes and my ordinances, then I will establish your royal throne over Israel forever, as I promised your father David, saying, 'There shall not fail you a successor on the throne of Israel.' If you turn aside from following me, you or your children, and do not keep my commandments and

my statutes that I have set before you, but go and serve other gods and worship them, then I will cut Israel off from the land that I have given them; and the house that I have consecrated for my name I will cast out of my sight; and Israel will become a proverb and a taunt among all peoples. (1 Kings 9:4–7)

Jerusalem – built as a city that is bound firmly together. To it the tribes go up, the tribes of the LORD, as was decreed for Israel, to give thanks to the name of the LORD. For there the thrones for judgement were set up, the thrones of the house of David. (Psalms 122:3–5) Cf. Psalm 132:13–17 for the ark of the covenant.

Brief commentary

(V. 1)
A rare moment of respite in the bellicose career of David.

(V. 2)
An implied intention.

(V. 5)
A rhetorical question, followed in the omitted text by a description of God as itinerant, always 'with' his wandering people. The tone in the next verse (not in our reading) is sarcastic really – does God *need* a house?

(V. 8)
This alludes to the call of David in 1 Samual 16:11.

(V. 9)
'Being with you' is almost a name for God in the Bible.

(V. 10)
A future promise based on past reality.

(V. 11)
God reviews the history of the Israelites. Punning on the word house

(meaning also, as in English, dynasty), God turns the tables on David.

(V. 16)
This promise lays the foundation of Jewish and later Christian hopes that God would send a descendant of David to shepherd his people again.

Pointers for prayer

a) The domestication of God is always a risk for believers, even though we know he is greater than our hearts and minds. Remember the moments when the sheer otherness of God was particularly real for you.

b) Another name for God in the Bible could be Ever Faithful. When have I been aware, in spite of all that was going on, that, yes, God was beside me all along? Thanksgiving.

c) The ark, symbol of God's roving presence, shows God not at all bound by structures, whether real or virtual, architectural or ecclesiastical. Hence we may say, in faith, that God is present to us fully, always, everywhere, no matter what. We are not always conscious of this and then, in certain moments, we are. Amen.

d) His kingdom will have no end – a prayer we say every Sunday in the Creed. The kingdom of God in Jesus' proclamation grounds all our hope.

Prayer

God ever faithful, show yourself again as constant love, always with us, even when we are not with you. Teach us to build our hopes on your foundations, that by setting aside our limited vision we may never take you for granted.

We make our prayer through our Lord Jesus Christ, your Son, who lives and reigns with you in the unity of the Holy Spirit, God for ever and ever. Amen.

Themes across the readings

The reading is essential background for the Annunciation, which mentions David explicitly in vv. 27 and 32 (v.33 – his kingdom will last for ever). The theme of God's fidelity to David (and his house) is a way of speaking of God's continued faithfulness and the continuity of God's revelation in Jesus. That is why David is so important in the New Testament.

In the Middle East, the churches, both Catholic and Orthodox, celebrate Old Testament saints in the liturgy, such as Moses, Elijah, Isaiah and David. (In the Western Church, only a few 'pre-Christian' figures make it, such as John the Baptist and his parents and Mary and her parents.) It is a mark of continuity and perhaps something we in the West could consider. These figures are immensely important in the New Testament and a good example would be David.

Without even trying to be pedantic (!), here is the full list of occurrences of 'David' across the New Testament. It may remind us of our Jewish roots. Matthew 1:1, 6, 17, 20; 9:27; 12:3, 23; 15:22; 20:30–31; 21:9, 15; 22:42–43, 45; Mark 2:25; 10:47–48; 11:10; 12:35–37; Luke 1:27, 32, 69; 2:4, 11; 3:31; 6:3; 18:38–39; 20:42, 44; John 7:42; Acts 1:16; 2:25, 29, 31, 34; 4:25; 7:45; 13:22, 34, 36; 15:16; Romans 1:3; 4:6; 11:9; 2 Timothy 2:8; Hebrews 4:7; 11:32; Revelation 3:7; 5:5; 22:16.

Chapter 5

Christmas Eve Vigil Mass ABC

Thought for the day

Tracing origins has always been of interest and nowadays it is possible to have a sample of your DNA tested to find out what kind of genetic mix you are. It can lead to (not always welcome) surprises! Jesus also had shadows in his genealogy, as is perfectly normal. There is hope, too, in the ancestors: God can write straight with our crooked lines. The shadows are not simply in our past, somehow in others then, but in each of us now as well. But the great message of the Gospel is that our past does not always have to stalk us – there is total forgiveness and even amnesia in God: *I, I am the one who blots out your rebellious deeds for my sake; your sins I do not remember* (Isaiah 43:25).

Prayer

Help us to accept from you, God, a new name, a new reality in Christ that we may know your forgiveness and love and be set free from our past sins and faults. Through Christ our Lord.

🌿 Gospel 🌿

Mt 1:1 An account of the genealogy of Jesus the Messiah, the son of David, the son of Abraham.

[2] Abraham was the father of Isaac, and Isaac the father of Jacob, and Jacob the father of Judah and his brothers, [3] and Judah the father of Perez and Zerah by Tamar, and Perez the father of Hezron, and Hezron the father of Aram, [4] and

Aram the father of Aminadab, and Aminadab the father of Nahshon, and Nahshon the father of Salmon, [5] and Salmon the father of Boaz by Rahab, and Boaz the father of Obed by Ruth, and Obed the father of Jesse, [6] and Jesse the father of King David.

And David was the father of Solomon by the wife of Uriah, [7] and Solomon the father of Rehoboam, and Rehoboam the father of Abijah, and Abijah the father of Asaph, [8] and Asaph the father of Jehoshaphat, and Jehoshaphat the father of Joram, and Joram the father of Uzziah, [9] and Uzziah the father of Jotham, and Jotham the father of Ahaz, and Ahaz the father of Hezekiah, [10] and Hezekiah the father of Manasseh, and Manasseh the father of Amos, and Amos the father of Josiah, [11] and Josiah the father of Jechoniah and his brothers, at the time of the deportation to Babylon.

[12] And after the deportation to Babylon: Jechoniah was the father of Salathiel, and Salathiel the father of Zerubbabel, [13] and Zerubbabel the father of Abiud, and Abiud the father of Eliakim, and Eliakim the father of Azor, [14] and Azor the father of Zadok, and Zadok the father of Achim, and Achim the father of Eliud, [15] and Eliud the father of Eleazar, and Eleazar the father of Matthan, and Matthan the father of Jacob, [16] and Jacob the father of Joseph the husband of Mary, of whom Jesus was born, who is called the Messiah.

[17] So all the generations from Abraham to David are fourteen generations; and from David to the deportation to Babylon, fourteen generations; and from the deportation to Babylon to the Messiah, fourteen generations.

[18] Now the birth of Jesus the Messiah took place in this way. When his mother Mary had been engaged to Joseph, but before they lived together, she was found to be with child from the Holy Spirit. [19] Her husband Joseph, being a righteous

man and unwilling to expose her to public disgrace, planned to dismiss her quietly. [20] But just when he had resolved to do this, an angel of the Lord appeared to him in a dream and said, 'Joseph, son of David, do not be afraid to take Mary as your wife, for the child conceived in her is from the Holy Spirit. [21] She will bear a son, and you are to name him Jesus, for he will save his people from their sins.' [22] All this took place to fulfil what had been spoken by the Lord through the prophet:

[23] 'Look, the virgin shall conceive and bear a son, and they shall name him Emmanuel,' which means, 'God is with us'.

[24] When Joseph awoke from sleep, he did as the angel of the Lord commanded him; he took her as his wife, [25] but had no marital relations with her until she had borne a son; and he named him Jesus.

Initial observations

There is no doubt that the (optional) genealogy is disconcerting for the modern reader/listener. Nevertheless it was clearly of immense significance for Matthew. By means of it, the evangelist was able to embed the story of Jesus in the story of God's first chosen people. It is likely that Matthew's community had just broken away from 'the synagogue'. At the same time, this community claimed to be in continuity with God's past disclosure to the Jewish people, now brought to completion in Jesus the Messiah. In particular, the figure of Moses (not mentioned here) dominates Matthew's presentation of Jesus.

Kind of writing

There are two kinds of writing here, genealogy and annunciation. The annunciation type-story shows this pattern:

1. appearance of an angel;
2. fear and/or prostration;
3. reassurance ('do not fear');

4. message;
5. objection;
6. a sign is given

The pattern is familiar from the Old Testament (*Ishmael* Genesis 16:7–12, *Isaac* Genesis 17:1–21; 18:1–12; *Samson* Judges 13:3–21) but is only partially present here in Matthew.

Old Testament background

The broad Old Testament story is presented schematically using the device of fourteen generations, taking us from Abraham, through David and the Exile to the time of Jesus. In antiquity, evidently, people were unaware of ovulation. As a result, women were omitted from genealogies. As a result the inclusion of women here is especially significant. Each one has a story.

Tamar: Genesis 38
Rahab: Joshua 2–6
Ruth: Ruth 1–4
Wife of Uriah (Bathsheba): 2 Samuel 11–12

All four are in some sense irregular, either sexually and/or as foreigners. They prepare for the great 'irregularity' of the virginal conception and look forward, at the same time, to the inclusion of the Gentiles in the new covenant in Jesus. Sinners likewise have a role in God's plan: three of the women are technically sinners, but so are lots of the men, such as David himself and Solomon.

(i) Joseph: The name Joseph reminds the aware bible reader of another Joseph in the book of Genesis.

(ii) Divorce was allowed by inference in Deuteronomy 24:1–4, although no biblical legislation formally permitted it.

(iii) Son of David: The relationship with David immediately calls to mind the guarantee and promise to the house of David made by the prophet Nathan in 2 Samuel 7 and the prayer version of it in Psalm 89.

(iv) Jesus is the Greek for Joshua, the name of Moses' successor, who actually led the people into the promised land. The name comes from

Hebrew/Aramaic and means 'YHWH is salvation' or 'YHWH saves/has saved'. As early Christians read the book of Joshua in Greek, they keep hearing the name Jesus/Joshua.

(v) The promise in Isaiah 7:14 is read as a messianic prophecy. In its original context, this text promised a successor to King Ahaz, born in the normal way.

(vi) Communication in a dream: The clear prototypes are Jacob (and his famous ladder) and Joseph (with his coat of many colours).

New Testament foreground

Now the eleven disciples went to Galilee, to the mountain to which Jesus had directed them. When they saw him, they worshipped him; but some doubted. And Jesus came and said to them, 'All authority in heaven and on earth has been given to me. Go therefore and make disciples of all nations, baptising them in the name of the Father and of the Son and of the Holy Spirit, and teaching them to obey everything that I have commanded you. And remember, *I am with you always*, to the end of the age.' (Matthew 28:16–20)

St Paul

For this reason it is by faith so that it may be by grace, with the result that the promise may be certain to all the descendants – not only to those who are under the law, but also to those who have the faith of Abraham, who is the father of us all (as it is written, 'I have made you the father of many nations'). He is our father in the presence of God whom he believed – the God who makes the dead alive and summons the things that do not yet exist as though they already do. Against hope Abraham believed in hope with the result that he became the father of many nations according to the pronouncement, 'so will your descendants be'. Without being weak in faith, he considered his own body as dead (because he was about one hundred years old) and the deadness of Sarah's womb. He did not waver in unbelief about the promise of God but was strengthened in faith, giving glory to God. (Romans 4:16–20)

Brief commentary

Because of the extended Old Testament background, only selected verses will be commented.

(V. 1)
The first verse anticipates the threefold pattern, pointing to Jesus.

(V. 6)
People did look back on the time of David as a sort of golden age and many hopes were expressed using Davidic imagery from the Psalms and other documents.

(V. 11)
The Babylonian Exile was a watershed in the history and imagination of the Jewish people. It will be referred to again in the slaughter of the innocents in Matthew 2:17–18.

(V. 16)
The pairing of a later Jacob with the later Joseph intentionally echoes the great patriarch, the father of Joseph, one of the twelve sons of Jacob, the progenitors of the twelve tribes of Israel.

(V. 17)
The writer insistently draws our attention to the pattern of fourteen. It may be significant that the consonants of the name David had the numerical value of fourteen in Hebrew.

(V. 18)
Mary was not descended from any of these people, but Joseph, as the legal father of Jesus, was. Betrothal was almost marriage; it was quite in order, therefore, to speak of divorce. The virginal conception is found also in Luke's account of the conception of Jesus.

(V. 20)
'Do not be afraid' is a key element in the Annunciation type-scene.

(V. 21)
As explained above the name Jesus means YHWH saves. In antiquity, names were regarded as key to the person's identity and mission (cf. *'nomen omen'*).

(Vv. 22–23)
Matthew peppers his account with fulfilment citations, of which this is the first. Originally, Isaiah 7:14 (in Hebrew) meant that a wife in the royal family would have a baby in the usual way. Matthew choose the Greek Old Testament (the Septuagint or the LXX) which speaks of a virgin conceiving, but again in the usual way. God-with-us will have a long echo in the Gospel.

(Vv. 24–25)
Joseph is always obedient (and silent) in Matthew 1–2.
Thus we learn that Jesus is a descendant of David, he will save the people from their sins and will be God-with-us.

Pointers for prayer

a) Every family tree casts shadows, shadows that can overshadow later generations. What have you learned about yourself from your family history?

b) In the narrative, Joseph faces a very challenging situation with a combination of kindness and logic, only to have both set aside by the surprise of God. Have you had that experience too?

c) God-with-us is a powerful expression, inviting me to reflect on my own experience of God with me in my life. Can I name any important moments of God's presence?

d) Every birth is a blessing – even my own! Am I still a blessing to those around me?

Prayer

God of Abraham and Sarah, of David and his descendants, unwearied is your love for us and steadfast is your covenant; wonderful beyond words is your gift of the Saviour, born of the Virgin Mary.

Count us among the people in whom you delight, and by this night's marriage of earth and heaven draw all generations into the embrace of your love.

We ask this through Jesus Christ, your Word made flesh, who lives and reigns with you in the unity of the Holy Spirit, in the splendour of eternal light, God for ever and ever. Amen.

🌿 Second Reading 🌿

Acts 13:16 So Paul stood up, gestured with his hand and said, 'Men of Israel, and you Gentiles who fear God, listen: [17] The God of this people Israel chose our ancestors and made the people great during their stay as foreigners in the country of Egypt, and with uplifted arm he led them out of it. [18] For a period of about forty years he put up with them in the wilderness. [19] After he had destroyed seven nations in the land of Canaan, he gave his people their land as an inheritance. [20] All this took about four hundred fifty years. After this he gave them judges until the time of Samuel the prophet. [21] Then they asked for a king, and God gave them Saul son of Kish, a man from the tribe of Benjamin, who ruled forty years. [22] After removing him, God raised up David their king. He testified about him: 'I have found David the son of Jesse to be a man after my heart, who will accomplish everything I want him to do.' [23] From the descendants of this man God brought to Israel a Saviour, Jesus, just as he promised. [24] Before Jesus arrived, John had proclaimed a baptism for repentance to all the people of Israel. [25] But while John was completing his mission, he said repeatedly, 'What do you think I am? I am not he. But look, one is coming after me. I am not worthy to untie the sandals on his feet!'

Initial observations

This unexpected and yet appropriate reading from the Acts of the Apostles places both John the Baptist and Jesus in the context of Israelite history. The mention of John in the vigil mass of Christmas resumes his role in the time of Advent and, at the same time, makes a bridge between the time of Advent and the present feast of Christmas.

Kind of writing

Fully fifty per cent of the Acts of the Apostles is made up sermons, discourses and letters. For example, speeches are given by Stephen, Cornelius, James, Gamaliel, Demetrius, Tertullus and Festus. In addition, Peter makes eight speeches, while Paul makes no fewer than nine (Acts 13:16–41; 14:15–17; 17:22–31; 20:18–35; 22:1–21; 24:10–21; 26:2–23, 25–27; 27:21–26; 28:17–20). While the speeches and sermons are adapted to the occasion and characters, we are really hearing Luke's theology of salvation history here. In the history writing of the time, it was up to the author to place appropriate speeches on the lips of the protagonists. As this is the very first of Paul's speeches, the first time we hear his 'voice', it is some way foundational and so especially important. It would be good to read the whole passage.

Origin of the reading

There are three large issues at stake here.

(i) John the Baptist was a continued source of anxiety, even for so late a gospel as Luke's. The evangelist goes to great trouble to 'locate' him in Luke 1–2 and to make sure we see him as the forerunner of Jesus.

(ii) The figure of David – a symbol of God's faithful across time to the people of Israel – was important for early Christianity and, evidently, for Jesus himself. Not only are we supposed to recall 2 Samuel 7, but also that David was seen as the author of the Psalms. In that capacity, early Christianity saw him as a prophet, foreseeing the time of the Messiah.

(iii) The Gospel of Luke and the Acts may have been written at a time when some Christians were rejecting the Jewish roots of the Christian project. Later in the second century, Marcion (a priest in Rome) challenged the use of Old Testament – he may have been the first but he was certainly not the last! The evangelist is very concerned, in both the Gospel and the Acts, to show continuity as a symbol of God's faithfulness through time.

Related passages

'Brothers, the scripture had to be fulfilled that the Holy Spirit foretold through *David* concerning Judas – who became the guide for those who arrested Jesus – for he was counted as one of us and received a share in this ministry.' (Acts 1:16–17)

But regarding the fact that he has raised Jesus from the dead, never again to be in a state of decay, God has spoken in this way: 'I will give you the holy and trustworthy promises made to *David*.' (Acts 13:34)

For David, after he had served God's purpose in his own generation, died, was buried with his ancestors, and experienced decay, but the one whom God raised up did not experience decay. (Acts 13:36–37)

The LORD declares to you that he himself will build a dynastic house for you. When the time comes for you to die, I will raise up your descendant, one of your own sons, to succeed you, and I will establish his kingdom. (2 Samuel 7:11–12)

Once and for all I have vowed by my own holiness, I will never deceive David. His dynasty will last forever. His throne will endure before me, like the sun, it will remain stable, like the moon, his throne will endure like the skies.' (Psalm 89:35–37)

Brief commentary

V. 1

Paul addresses two distinct groups: fellow Jews and 'god–fearers', that is, Gentiles attracted to Judaism. Such a group is known from literature and from archaeology and they may have been drawn to Judaism on account of its pure monotheism, high ethics and noble antiquity.

V. 17

Paul cannot tell the story of Jesus without reference to the central story of the Pentateuch, the Exodus. The use of the third person (they) is revealing about the time of writing, indicating already some level of detachment.

Vv. 18–21

These verses are omitted for reasons of brevity but are essential for the coherence of the whole story.

V. 22

Paul is made to abbreviate the familiar and wonderful story of the search for a successor to Saul. David is praised extravagantly: *a man after my heart, who will carry out all my wishes.*

V. 23

The promise takes us back to 2 Samuel 7 and Psalm 89 (see above).

V. 24

This is a summary of both Luke 1–2 and Luke 3:1–17.

V. 25

This fits with the way Luke has timed the baptism of Jesus in his gospel: Luke 3:19–21. It is made clear for the nth time that John is not the Messiah.

Pointers for prayer

a) Each of us has a story but it is never just our own. On the contrary, we are part of a stream, a continuity. My story too is embedded in the generations before me, in the Christian story, and that story is itself embedded in the story of Israel.

b) God wants all of us to be people 'after my heart, who will carry out all my wishes'. What do I do to make my heart transparent to the will of God?

c) The sense of preparation and excitement is tangible as Christmas comes around. What are my hopes this year?

Prayer

May we feel this year, O Lord, the passion and longing of John the Baptist and so prepare ourselves to mark the birth of Jesus, son of David, Son of Man, Son of God, who lives and reigns for ever and ever. Amen.

🌿 First Reading 🌿

Is 62:1 'For the sake of Zion I will not be silent;
for the sake of Jerusalem I will not be quiet,
until her vindication shines brightly
and her deliverance burns like a torch.'

2   Nations will see your vindication,
and all kings your splendour.
You will be called by a new name
that the LORD himself will give you.

3   You will be a majestic crown in the hand of the LORD,
a royal turban in the hand of your God.

4   You will no longer be called, 'Abandoned',
and your land will no longer be called 'Desolate'.
Indeed, you will be called 'My Delight is in Her',
and your land 'Married'.
For the LORD will take delight in you,
and your land will be married to him.

5   As a young man marries a young woman,
so your sons will marry you.
As a bridegroom rejoices over a bride,
so your God will rejoice over you.

Initial observations

Our readings open with a passage full of joy and hope, very suitable for
the season. It is not quite unfettered happiness but at the same time it is
a thrilling passage. The psalm going with the reading joins the uplifting
vision of Isaiah with more traditional hopes rooted in God's faithfulness
to David and his dynasty. As a result the psalm, rather than the Isaiah
reading, sets up the imagery which will be important for both the Acts
and Matthew.

Kind of writing

Isaiah 62 is a prayer for the restoration of Jerusalem, which really runs from 61:10 to 62:12. Our excerpts shows clearly the use of 'twin lines', or parallelism, so much part of the energy and power of biblical poetry.

Origin of the reading

Our passage is taken from Third Isaiah and was written most likely in the years after the return from Exile, following the arrival of Cyrus of Persia in 539 BC. Hopes were high after the exiles came back but the reconstruction was frustratingly slow. Accordingly, the prophet gives a great message of hope, to encourage the despondent. Some of the pain is found even in this happy poem: forsaken and desolate. It is evident that much remained to be achieved.

The reading is, nevertheless, very fitting for the vigil Mass of Christmas on account of the tone of expectation combined with sheer joy, spilling over into the exuberant.

Related passages

'Indeed, the LORD will call you back like a wife who has been abandoned and suffers from depression, like a young wife when she has been rejected,' says your God. (Isaiah 54:6)

The LORD has proclaimed to the end of the earth: 'Say to daughter Zion, "See, your salvation comes; his reward is with him, and his recompense before him." They shall be called, "The Holy People, The Redeemed of the Lord"; and you shall be called, "Sought Out, A City Not Forsaken".' (Isaiah 62:11–12)

Brief commentary

(V. 1a)
The prophet is unable to keep silent. The parallel lines are uneasily synonymous: Zion is part of Jerusalem; 'keep silent' becomes 'rest.'

(V. 1b)

Note how vindication (= God acting justly) and salvation are in parallel. At dawn, the day has broken, but the burning torch suggests it is still night. So, not quite there yet!

(V. 2a)

The parallel lines shift now from vindication to glory, that is, to the public acknowledgement of God's action.

(V. 2b)

In the culture, a change of name is a change of being or relationship ('*nomen omen*'). The parallelism is interrupted to give the origin of the new name: God himself. Cf. *One will say, 'I belong to the* Lord,*' and another will use the name "Jacob". 'One will write on his hand, "The* Lord's*", 'and use the name "Israel".'* (Isaiah 44:5).

(V. 3)

Royal symbolism is used, facilitating the change of focus in the psalm to David.

(V. 4a)

The true feelings and experiences of the listeners come to expression. Cf. 'Zion said, "The Lord has abandoned me, the sovereign master has forgotten me"' (Isaiah 49:14).   'Indeed, the Lord will call you back like a wife who has been abandoned and suffers from depression, like a young wife when she has been rejected,' says your God (Isaiah 54:6).

(V. 4b–c)

V. 4a is turned around and robustly positive language is used. Cf. *Jerusalem will bring me joy, and my people will bring me happiness. The sound of weeping or cries of sorrow will never be heard in her again.* (Isaiah 65:19) V. 4b is 'activated' so to speak in 4c. It is not just a change of name but a change of reality, of being, of heart.

(V. 5a)

The parallelism is evident. Why builder? A more literal translation runs as follows: *As a youth espouses a maiden, Your sons shall espouse you* (Isaiah 62:5 Jewish Publication Translation). The word 'son' is related to the word 'to build'. Respecting the parallelism, evidently, the New Jerusalem translates thus: *Like a young man marrying a virgin, your rebuilder will wed you, and as the bridegroom rejoices in his bride, so will your God rejoice in you* (Isaiah 62:5 *New Jerusalem Bible*).

(V. 5b)
This is an uncommon and unexpected metaphor. It reminds one of Psalm 19: *In the sky he has pitched a tent for the sun. Like a bridegroom it emerges from its chamber; like a strong man it enjoys running its course* (Psalm 19:4–5).

Pointers for prayer

a) We do not often think of God as 'rejoicing', much less rejoicing over us or even over me. We touch the heart of the incarnation: 'Thus we are writing these things so that our joy may be complete' (1 John 1:4).

b) Not being able to hold it in was also the experience of Jeremiah (6:11). Do I feel any such 'compulsion' to let others into the secret?

Prayer

God, truly you rejoice in yourself, in your cosmos and even in each one of us. Teach us to live by such conviction that our faith may be truly alive and that others may be drawn to life abundant. Through Christ our Lord. Amen.

Themes across the readings

The figure of David, in the psalm, second reading and gospel, brings all these readings together. The fidelity of God to the Davidic dynasty symbolises God's faithfulness to us all across time. That faithfulness reaches a new stage in Jesus, a descendant of David. As Christ-believers, we are invited to look back over the major stages and events in our own lives and see how God has always been there for us.

Chapter 6

Christmas Eve Midnight Mass ABC

Thought for the day

The birth of any child is always a source of wonder, when we feel nearer to the mystery of life and, in a most natural way, the mystery of God brought near. In the birth of Jesus, we see our God made visible and so are caught up in love of the God we cannot see. The thrilling reality of the Word made flesh is both gift and call. In the words of the first letter of John, *Beloved, since God loved us so much, we also ought to love one another* (1 John 4:11). We are challenged to love the God we cannot see in the neighbour we can see. There can be no separation of these two realities: to love God is to love your neighbour and to love your neighbour is to love God.

Prayer

Today love itself became flesh like one of us, so that you, O God, might see and love in us what you see and love in him. May we see you and love you in our brothers and sisters. Through Christ our Lord.

🌿 Gospel 🌿

Lk 2:1 In those days a decree went out from Emperor Augustus that all the world should be registered. [2] This was the first registration and was taken while Quirinius was governor of Syria. [3] All went to their own towns to be registered. [4] Joseph also went from the town of Nazareth in Galilee to Judea, to the city of David called Bethlehem, because he was descended from the house and family of David. [5] He went to be registered with Mary, to whom he was engaged and who was expecting a child. [6] While they were there, the time came for her to deliver her child. [7] And she gave birth to her firstborn son and wrapped him in bands of cloth, and laid him in a manger, because there was no place for them in the inn.

[8] In that region there were shepherds living in the fields, keeping watch over their flock by night. [9] Then an angel of the Lord stood before them, and the glory of the Lord shone around them, and they were terrified. [10] But the angel said to them, 'Do not be afraid; for see – I am bringing you good news of great joy for all the people: [11] to you is born this day in the city of David a Saviour, who is the Messiah, the Lord. [12] This will be a sign for you: you will find a child wrapped in bands of cloth and lying in a manger.' [13] And suddenly there was with the angel a multitude of the heavenly host, praising God and saying, [14] 'Glory to God in the highest heaven, and on earth peace among those whom he favours!'

Initial observations

The birth stories of Jesus are found only in Matthew and Luke, as is well known. Like all gospel stories, they are written retrospectively in the light of the resurrection. Again, just as in the Prologue of John, they serve to provide a Christological key to the identity of Jesus in the rest of the narrative. Finally, again like the Prologue, they establish a significant level of continuity with the revelation to God's first chosen people. Both Matthew and Luke write in dialogue with patterns and personalities from the Old Testament and, to a high degree, the writing is determined by those earlier models. While there is indeed a historical core (the Holy Family, Nazareth, Bethlehem, Jerusalem, Herod), nevertheless these accounts are 'parabolic' (even *haggadic*) in nature rather than straight history as we would understand it today.

Kind of writing

In the context of the culture, this is 'historical' writing, mirroring the conventions and practices of the time. In such cases, the writers use commonplaces, to express the significance of the person being written about. The goal is to proclaim the present, living Jesus and not merely to present the past.

Two backgrounds need to be considered, Jewish and Greco-Roman.

(i) *Midrashic* commentary was a form of filling in the gaps, answering questions that the Scripture itself did not make clear. Accordingly, we might consider certain of the apocryphal writings under the same rubric.

The Greek works of Philo and Josephus (especially in his *Jewish Antiquities*) also expand the biblical text, fill in gaps, allegorise, and otherwise interpret the Bible in ways reminiscent of the rabbis. Many of the traditions that these Jews quote in their interpretations of Jewish Scripture find parallels in rabbinic *midrash*.

Neither Matthew 1–2 nor Luke 1–2 is strictly *midrash*, however. *Haggadah* was another kind of devotional writing designed to instruct and uplift. The strong links to biblical models and motifs lend a very strong biblical air to the writing.

(ii) In Greco-Roman culture, the birth of a ruler is sometimes celebrated with a list of his (future) benefits to all humanity. For example, the Priene Calendar Inscription includes some breathtaking affirmation about Augustus, the first emperor:

Since providence, which has divinely disposed our lives, having employed zeal and ardour, has arranged the most perfect culmination for life by producing Augustus, whom for the benefit of mankind she has filled with excellence, as if she had granted him as a saviour for us and our descendants, a saviour who brought war to an end and set all things in peaceful order, and since with his appearance, Caesar exceeded the hopes of all those who had received good news before us, not only surpassing those who had been benefactors before him, but not even leaving any hope of surpassing him for those who are to come in the future, and since the beginning of the good news on his account for the world was the birthday of a god …

Old Testament background

> I was nursed with care in swaddling cloths. (Wisdom 7:4)

> An ox recognises its owner, a donkey recognises where its owner puts its food; but Israel does not recognise me, my people do not understand. (Isaiah 1:3)

> As for you, Bethlehem Ephrathah, seemingly insignificant among the clans of Judah – from you a king will emerge who will rule over Israel on my behalf, one whose origins are in the distant past. (Micah 5:2)

> For a child has been born to us, a son has been given to us. He shoulders responsibility and is called: Extraordinary Strategist, Mighty God, Everlasting Father, Prince of Peace. (Isaiah 9:6)

> How delightful it is to see approaching over the mountains the feet of a messenger who announces peace, a messenger who brings good news, who announces deliverance, who says to Zion, 'Your God reigns!' (Isaiah 52:7)

New Testament foreground

Men of Israel, listen to these words: Jesus the Nazarene, a man clearly attested to you by God with powerful deeds, wonders and miraculous signs that God performed among you through him, just as you yourselves know – this man, who was handed over by the predetermined plan and foreknowledge of God, you executed by nailing him to a cross at the hands of Gentiles. But God raised him up, having released him from the pains of death, because it was not possible for him to be held in its power. (Acts 2:22–24)

St Paul

From Paul, a slave of Christ Jesus, called to be an apostle, set apart for the gospel of God. This gospel he promised beforehand through his prophets in the holy scriptures, concerning his Son who was a descendant of David with reference to the flesh, who was appointed the Son-of-God-in-power according to the Holy Spirit by the resurrection from the dead, Jesus Christ our Lord. Through him we have received grace and our apostleship to bring about the obedience of faith among all the Gentiles on behalf of his name. You also are among them, called to belong to Jesus Christ. To all those loved by God in Rome, called to be saints: Grace and peace to you from God our Father and the Lord Jesus Christ! (Romans 1:1–7)

Brief commentary

(V. 1)

Augustus was the grand–nephew and adopted son of the deified Julius Caesar, and therefore could claim to be a 'son of God', a *dei filius*. On his death in AD 14, Tiberius became emperor. There was no *worldwide* census in the time of Augustus. Luke is mixing it up with a census of Syria, which took place before the death of Archelaus in AD 6, under the governorship of Quirinius. The solemn beginning resembles 3:1. Augustus was regarded as the saviour of the world and the bringer of the Pax Romana. Luke challenges that, especially in 2:14.

(V. 2)

Publius Sulpicius Quirinius was a real historical figure, from Lanuvio (Lanuvium), not far from Castelgandolfo, who was made legate of Syria in AD 6 with the special task of restructuring Judea as a Roman province.

(V. 3)

There is no evidence for such a disruptive practice. It does, however, echo the instructions for the Jubilee Year, a theme in Luke 4:16–30.

(V. 4)

City of David would normally be taken to be Jerusalem; here, of course, it refers to Bethlehem.

(V. 5)

This is a quick summary of Luke 1:26–38.

(V. 6)
Cf. Genesis 25:24 and Luke 1:57.

(V. 7)
'Firstborn' meant a particular status in the Jewish Law, without preju-
dice to other children being born. The old word 'swaddle' is a direct echo
of Wisdom 7:4, where the whole context is interesting. Solomon, *son
of David*, was also wrapped in swaddling clothes. The reference to the
manger was filled out in the iconographic tradition to cause an unkind
echo of Isaiah 1:3. It can mean a variety of things: a private home, a
room, an inn, a space in a stable.

(V. 8)
The shepherd echoes the David tradition. This has also been used to
date the actual birth of Jesus to between March and November, when
shepherds would be out in the fields. Shepherds were sometimes considered outcasts. Bethlehem: cf. Micah 4–5, especially 5:2 (above).

(V. 9)
Glory: cf. Luke 2:9, 14, 32; 4:6; 9:26, 31–32; 12:27; 14:10; 17:18; 19:38;
21:27; 24:26. Shone: cf. the conversion of St Paul in Acts 26:13.

(V. 10)
'Do not be afraid' is a commonplace of angelic appearances and theoph-
anies. The long English expression 'bring good news' is a single verb in
Greek, 'I gospel you', so to speak.

(V. 11)
'Today' is a favourite expression of Luke. Cf. Luke 2:11; 4:21; 5:26;
12:28; 13:32–33; 19:5, 9; 22:34, 61; 23:43. Saviour is unexpectedly rare
in the gospels and Acts: Matthew (0), Mark (0), Luke (2), John (1), Acts
(2). (Cf. Luke 1:47; 2:11; John 4:42; Acts 5:31; 13:23). Christ the Lord
(common in Paul) is rare in the gospels and Acts: Matthew (0), Mark
(0), Luke (2), John (0), Acts (1).

(V. 12)
Jesus, not Augustus, is the saviour. Cf. Isaiah 9:6 and 52:7.

(V. 13)

Luke regularly underlines the praise of God: Matthew (0), Mark (0), Luke (6), John (0).

(V. 14)

Glory is the visible manifestation of divine majesty and a strong contrast with the fragility of a newborn baby. Highest heavens, i.e. into the further reaches of heaven, so to speak.

Pointers for prayer

a) Bring to mind a time when the birth of a child made a huge impact on you. Use the experience to meditate upon the birth of Jesus, the incarnation.

a) There is great joy in the gospel tonight. Have you ever felt such spontaneous, exultant happiness? A prayer of praise and thanksgiving.

Prayer

Good and gracious God, on this holy night you gave us your Son, the Lord of the universe, wrapped in swaddling clothes, the Saviour of all, lying in a manger. On this holy night draw us into the mystery of your love. Join our voices with the heavenly host, that we may sing your glory on high.

Give us a place among the shepherds, that we may find the one for whom we have waited, Jesus Christ, your Word made flesh, who lives and reigns with you in the unity of the Holy Spirit, in the splendour of eternal light, God for ever and ever. Amen.

🌿 Second Reading 🌿

Tit 2:11 For the grace of God has appeared, bringing salvation to all people. [12] It trains us to reject godless ways and worldly desires and to live self-controlled, upright and godly lives in the present age, [13] as we wait for the happy fulfilment of our hope in the glorious appearing of our great God and Saviour, Jesus Christ. [14] He gave himself for us to set us free from every kind of lawlessness and to purify for himself a people who are truly his, who are eager to do good. [15] *So communicate these* *things with the sort of exhortation or rebuke that carries full authority. Don't let anyone look down on you.*

Initial observations

Our reading is beautifully laid out and teaches us that, as Christians, we live in the in-between time, our lives marked by both memory and hope. It is chosen today because it underlines that salvation is for all, without distinction. The claims about Jesus put the writer on a collision course with the Empire (see below).

Many scholars think this letter does not come from the hand of the apostle himself. Titus is a document of the second or even third generation of the Pauline churches.

Kind of writing

The Pastorals present themselves as personal letters from Paul to significant companions. In reality, they are written to communities (in Asia Minor) to bring Pauline doctrine into a new context. They preserve, however, the letter structure, as in the case of Titus:

> 1:1–4 Salutation
> 1:5–3:11 Body of the letter
> 3:12–15 Travels, greetings, blessing

The body of the letter:

> 1:5–9 Elders
> 1:10–16 Warnings
> 2:1–10 The Christian household
> 2:11–15 *Appearance of Christ*
> 3:1–11 To the whole church

For completeness' sake, v. 15 is added (it does capture the different tone of these documents). Some of the resounding vocabulary used here marks the text as *not* from Paul: to appear; saving (= salvation as an adjective); to renounce; worldly; self–controlled (= lit. wisely); godly; manifestation; great; to redeem; of his own; to look down on (none of these expressions is ever found in the undisputed letters of Paul).

Origin of the reading

The writer(s) of the Pastorals were facing a variety of threats at the start of the second century. In response, it is true that there is some domestication of the radical Paul but there is more to it than that.

The letters also represent a development of Pauline doctrine in several directions: (i) spirits, angels and the Holy Spirit; (ii) the Church as the household of God, with great regard for the inspired Jewish Scriptures. The tension towards the end of time found in Paul is abandoned – there will still be a second coming, but it is in the very indefinite future. As for date and place, mostly likely it comes from Asia Minor/Western Turkey, around the year AD 100.

Related passages

> But as for you, continue in what you have learned and firmly believed, knowing from whom you learned it, and how from childhood you have known the sacred writings that are able to instruct you for salvation through faith in Christ Jesus. (2 Timothy 3:14–15)

> Paul, a servant of God and an apostle of Jesus Christ, for the sake of the faith of God's elect and the knowledge of the truth that is in accordance with godliness, in the hope of eternal life that God, who never lies, promised before the ages began – in due time he revealed his word through the proclamation with which I have been entrusted by the command of God our Saviour, to Titus, my loyal child in the faith we share: Grace and peace from God the Father and Christ Jesus our Saviour. (Titus 1:1–4)

> But when the goodness and loving kindness of God our Saviour appeared, he saved us, not because of any works of righteousness that we had done, but according to his mercy, through the water of rebirth and renewal by the Holy Spirit. This Spirit he poured out on us richly through Jesus Christ our Saviour, so that, having been justified by his grace, we might become heirs according to the hope of eternal life. (Titus 3:4–7)

Brief commentary

(V. 11)

The grace of God is evidently bringing salvation to all; it is not limited to one people (for example, the Jews) or to an elite (for example, Gnostics). At the heart of this first appearance stands the cross and resurrection.

(V. 12)

This pile-up of attitudes teaches us that we are to live truly transformed lives in response to this great grace. The Christmas feast can be cosy and 'harmless'. Taking it earnestly means embarking on a journey of deep change. The gospel is an all-or-nothing offer of life transformed.

(V. 13)

There will be a second appearance or coming. The Gospel is lived in hope between these events. 'Great God and Saviour' was found in Ephesus in an inscription dedicated to Caesar. For the author of Titus, the Gospel proclaims another great God and saviour, Jesus Christ.

(V. 14)

There are allusions here to the authentic Paul in 1 Thessalonians 2:15–21. The 'for us' indicates that not everyone has responded; it is also an echo of the Suffering Servant theme. The biblical language of chosen people etc. is applied here to the Christian community. Again, a transformed life is indicated.

Pointers for prayer

a) At Christmas, once we get past the tinsel, we encounter 'the scandalous particularity of the incarnation' at the heart of Christian faith. Who is Jesus in my life? How do I experience his salvation?

b) As we get older, we gradually get used to living in between birth and death; there is for us another in-between: the fact of Christ and hope we have in him. This is the basis for our transformed living in the present moment.

Prayer

Saving, healing God, you reach out to us in Jesus, bringing light into the darkness of human life. Help us put our hands into his hands, that he may bring us to you.

Grant this through him, whose light has shone, your Son, our Lord Jesus Christ, who lives and reigns with you in the unity of the Holy Spirit, God, for ever and ever. Amen

❧ First Reading ❧

Is 9:1 *But there will be no gloom for those who were in anguish. In the former time he brought into contempt the land of Zebulun and the land of Naphtali, but in the latter time he will make glorious the way of the sea, the land beyond the Jordan, Galilee of the nations.*

2   The people who walked in darkness
             have seen a great light;
         those who lived in a land of deep darkness –
             on them light has shined.

3   You have multiplied the nation,
             you have increased its joy;
         they rejoice before you
             as with joy at the harvest,
             as people exult when dividing plunder.

4   For the yoke of their burden,
             and the bar across their shoulders,
             the rod of their oppressor,
             you have broken as on the day of Midian.

5   For all the boots of the tramping warriors
             and all the garments rolled in blood
             shall be burned as fuel for the fire.

6   For a child has been born for us,
             a son given to us;
         authority rests upon his shoulders;
             and he is named

> Wonderful Counsellor, Mighty God,
>   Everlasting Father, Prince of Peace.
> 7 His authority shall grow continually,
>   and there shall be endless peace
> for the throne of David and his kingdom.
>   He will establish and uphold it
> with justice and with righteousness
>   from this time onward and for ever more.
> The zeal of the LORD of hosts will do this.

Initial observations

This is an especially appropriate and loved reading for Christmas Midnight Mass and the setting of parts of this text in Handel's *Messiah* have made it even more familiar and appreciated. The themes of darkness/light, child and the throne of David fit the feast. Nevertheless, it does come from a particular moment in history and has to be read first of all in its religious and political setting.

Kind of writing

Isaiah 9:2–7 is a prophetic oracle in the form of poetry, reflecting the conventions and techniques of biblical poetry generally. The parallelism is evident, for instance, in vv. 2ab and 2cd. As the verses proceed, there is insistence by sheer force of repetition. Thus in v. 3, we have joy, rejoice, exult. The suggestion of dividing plunder (after an implied victory) at the end of v. 3 is continued in the military metaphors of vv. 4 and 5. Thus a reversal of a national calamity is envisaged. What has brought this about? The birth of an heir to the family of David. Tremendous hopes are placed on the shoulders of this child. Of course, there is no way of knowing that a child would have been able to achieve all this. Instead, the birth is taken to be a mark of God's continued fidelity to the house of David and the salvation to God will be the work of God himself. In all the colourful imagery in vv. 6–7, important words are profiled: peace, justice, righteousness.

Origin of the reading

As noted elsewhere, the present book of Isaiah reflects three distinct periods. The original Isaiah of Jerusalem was active from about 738 BC (Isaiah 6: 1) until 701 BC, perhaps until 687/6 BC, i.e. a considerable ministry of some forty or fifty years. His preaching is preserved in Isaiah 1–39. The period was a time of transition from prosperity and security to insecurity and threat as the Assyrian empire flexed its muscles. In the time of Isaiah, there were several conflicts with Assyria: 743–738, 735–732 (the Syro-Ephraimite war), 714–705 and, finally, 703–701.

Our excerpt comes from the period of the Syro-Ephraimite war. During this time, Isaiah preached the uncomfortable view that the Assyrians, under the marvellously named Tiglath-Pileser III, were an instrument of God, sent to punish and to bring Israel back to true faith in YHWH. Isaiah 1–12 deals with the condemnation of Judah (through Assyria) and God's offer of salvation through renewed fidelity. The cycles of promise (2–4) and threat (5–11) are interrupted by Isaiah 6:1–9:7, made up of oracles dealing with the Syro-Ephraimite war. This block forms the core of Isaiah 2–12 and provides the theological heart of the chapters. The traditions about Zion and the Davidic monarchy are expounded and explored. The typical pattern is threat, punishment, salvation.

Related passages

Several passages, too long to cite, come to mind: 2 Samuel 7; Isaiah 2:4, 7:14; 11:1–2, 8–9.

> He shall judge between the nations, and shall arbitrate for many peoples; they shall beat their swords into ploughshares, and their spears into pruning hooks; nation shall not lift up sword against nation, neither shall they learn war any more (Isaiah 2:4). Therefore the Lord himself will give you a sign. Look, the young woman is with child and shall bear a son, and shall name him Immanuel (Isaiah 7:14). A shoot shall come out from the stump of Jesse, and a branch shall grow out of his roots. The spirit of the LORD shall rest on him,

the spirit of wisdom and understanding, the spirit of counsel and might, the spirit of knowledge and the fear of the LORD. The nursing child shall play over the hole of the asp, and the weaned child shall put its hand on the adder's den. They will not hurt or destroy on all my holy mountain; for the earth will be full of the knowledge of the LORD as the waters cover the sea (Isaiah 11:1–2, 8–9).

Brief commentary

(V. 2)
Darkness represents the calamity that has befallen the kingdom of Judah; light is used for deliverance through a new king 'of David's line'.

(V. 3)
God is addressed ('you') and given the credit for the restored community, leading to great rejoicing. A contrast is drawn in which harvest points to the fruits of labour while plunder points to the fruits of conflict already over.

(V. 4)
Note the emphasis: yoke, bar, rod. In Judges 7–8, Gideon's victory over Midian delivered the people from foreign oppression.

(V. 5)
An end to war is pictured here. Cf. *He shall judge between the nations, and shall arbitrate for many peoples; they shall beat their swords into ploughshares, and their spears into pruning hooks; nation shall not lift up sword against nation, neither shall they learn war any more* (Isaiah 2:4).

(V. 6)
The historical referent is a child born of Davidic ancestry. 'Mighty God' might seem too much for a human being, but the New American Bible translated 'God–hero'. In any case: wisdom, heroism, fatherhood, peace. Prince of peace because the king establishes a safe socio-economic environment for his people.

(V. 7)
Peace is emphasised again. The import of the very last line has been well

captured in the New English Translation: *The Lord's intense devotion to his people will accomplish this.* This 'zeal' is a covenant quality of God in relation to Israel.

Pointers for prayer

a) Recall times when you have 'walked in darkness'. What was it like? What helped you to keep going? Was there a turning point, when darkness turned to light?

b) A birth is always a joy! Think of the joy of your own parents when you yourself arrived in the world. Use this very natural human happiness to come close to the happiness of today's feast.

c) Endless peace sounds great, but, as we know, peace is always 'under construction', always fragile, always in need of support. Where have you experienced peace? What about your own commitment to be a peacemaker, a bearer of peace to others?

Prayer

Loving God, our light and our hope, show yourself once more as our true guide. Teach us to recognise in your Son Jesus love which you alone give, the peace the world cannot give. Amen.

Themes across the readings

By means of the response, the first reading is read in the light of Jesus' birth and appearing, themes taken up in the second reading and the gospel. There is an air of excitement and joy, of hope finally fulfilled. The thrill of every human birth should help us celebrate the birth of our saviour.

Chapter 7

Christmas Day Dawn Mass ABC

Thought for the day

Sharing the excitement is a very human response. We have all done it at some stage: some great news in the family, perhaps at a promotion or the discovery of a place of spectacular beauty or some situation that has turned around. The desire to let others know tells us that sharing such experiences is itself part of the original delight. Something similar may be said of the sense of discovery and delight we find in the Good News of Jesus. Like the prophets of old (Jeremiah 20:9) or St Paul (1 Corinthians 9:16), we just can't keep it in! We want, we *need* to let others know in order to complete our delight and our sense of discovery.

Prayer

In these days, loving God, give us not only courageous joy but joyful courage to proclaim to others our own delight at the discovery of Good News.
May we be bearers of your Word of life to all.
Through the same Christ our Lord. Amen.

✤ Gospel ✤

Lk 2:15 When the angels had left them and gone into heaven, the shepherds said to one another, 'Let us go now to Bethlehem and see this thing that has taken place, which the Lord has made known to us.' [16] So they went with haste and found Mary and Joseph, and the child lying in the manger. [17] When they saw this, they made known what had been told them about this child; [18] and all who heard it were amazed at what the shepherds told them. [19] But Mary treasured all these words and pondered them in her heart. [20] The shepherds returned, glorifying and praising God for all they had heard and seen, as it had been told them.

Initial observations

This reading is simply the continuation of the reading for Midnight Mass. Some of the information given there applies here too, of course. It illustrates a response to the events of salvation and already some are worshipping the baby.

Kind of writing

(i) History: In the context of the culture, this is 'historical' writing, mirroring the conventions and practices of the time. In such cases, the writers use standard common places or *topoi* to express the significance of the person being written about. As can be seen in the notes, the history is a bit dodgy and the place given to the miraculous would not count as history today.

(ii) *Midrash*: Neither Matthew 1–2 nor Luke 1–2 is strictly *midrash*, a type of rewriting and filling out of biblical narratives found at the time. However, the strong links to biblical models and motifs lend a kind of midrashic air to the writing.

Old Testament background

(i) David as shepherd: 'When they came, he looked on Eliab and thought, "Surely the Lord's anointed is now before the Lord." But the Lord said to Samuel, "Do not look on his appearance or on the height of his stature, because I have rejected him; for the Lord does not see as mortals see; they look on the outward appearance, but the Lord looks on the heart." Then Jesse called Abinadab, and made him pass before Samuel. He said, "Neither has the Lord chosen this one." Then Jesse made Shammah pass by. And he said, "Neither has the Lord chosen this one." Jesse made seven of his sons pass before Samuel, and

Samuel said to Jesse, "The Lord has not chosen any of these." Samuel said to Jesse, "Are all your sons here?" And he said, "There remains yet the youngest, but he is keeping the sheep." And Samuel said to Jesse, "Send and bring him; for we will not sit down until he comes here." He sent and brought him in. Now he was ruddy, and had beautiful eyes, and was handsome. The Lord said, "Rise and anoint him; for this is the one." Then Samuel took the horn of oil, and anointed him in the presence of his brothers; and the spirit of the Lord came mightily upon David from that day forward. Samuel then set out and went to Ramah' (1 Samuel 16:6–13).

(ii) Davidic shepherd to come: 'I will set up over them one shepherd, my servant David, and he shall feed them: he shall feed them and be their shepherd' (Ezekiel 34:23). 'My servant David shall be king over them; and they shall all have one shepherd. They shall follow my ordinances and be careful to observe my statutes' (Ezekiel 37:24).

(iii) Bethlehem: Often mentioned in connection with David (1 Samuel 17:12, 15; 20:6, 28; 2 Samuel 23:14–16; 1 Chronicles 11:16–18; Luke 2:4; John 7:42). A significant echo can also be found in the book of Ruth (Ruth 1:1–2, 19, 22; 2:4; 4:11). The key text, however, is the one cited by Luke: 'But you, O Bethlehem of Ephrathah, who are one of the little clans of Judah, from you shall come forth for me one who is to rule in Israel, whose origin is from of old, from ancient days' (Micah 5:2).

New Testament foreground

The Davidic origin of Jesus is important in the New Testament and present in the earliest texts, such as Romans 1:1–7. It is important in the gospels and is present even in John's Gospel. David is a consistent subject of reflection in Luke's second volume also. For example:

The whole assembly kept silence, and listened to Barnabas and Paul as they told of all the signs and wonders that God had done through them among the Gentiles. After they finished speaking, James replied, 'My brothers, listen to me. Simeon has related how God first looked favourably on the Gentiles, to take from among them a people for his name. This agrees with the words of the prophets, as it is written, 'After this I will return, and I will rebuild the dwelling of David, which has fallen; from its ruins I will rebuild it, and I will set it up, so that all other peoples may seek the Lord – even all the Gentiles over whom my name has been called. Thus says the Lord, who has been making these things known from long ago.' (Acts 15:12–19)

And now, friends, I know that you acted in ignorance, as did also your rulers. In this way God fulfilled what he had foretold through all the prophets, that his Messiah would suffer. Repent therefore, and turn to God so that your sins may be wiped out, so that times of refreshing may come from the presence of the Lord, and that he may send the Messiah appointed for you, that is, Jesus, who must remain in heaven until the time of universal restoration that God announced long ago through his holy prophets. (Acts 3:17–21).

St Paul

Apart from Romans 1:1–7, Paul refers to David as the author of the Psalms. So also David speaks of the blessedness of those to whom God reckons righteousness apart from works: 'Blessed are those whose iniquities are forgiven, and whose sins are covered; blessed is the one against whom the Lord will not reckon sin.' (Romans 4:6–8)

Brief commentary

(V. 15)
Shepherds as such don't really recur in the Gospel. But there is, of course, the parable of the lost sheep in Luke 15:3–7.

(V. 16)
Mary and Joseph were previously mentioned in Luke 1:27.

(V. 17)
The word for what had been told them (*rhēma*) is a feature of Luke–

Acts: Matthew (5); Mark (2); Luke (9); John (12); Acts (14). The range is from 'what was said' to 'an event that can be spoken about'. That is, they bear witness, confirming their experience. Cf. Luke 24:35.

(V. 18)

The 'all' is very important for Matthew and for Luke and on this day means that salvation is offered to all without discrimination or distinction. Here are the occurrences: Matthew (129); Mark (69); Luke (158); John (65); Acts (171). Cf. 'In the last days it will be, God declares, that I will pour out my Spirit upon all flesh, and your sons and your daughters shall prophesy, and your young men shall see visions, and your old men shall dream dreams' (Acts 2:17). 'Then Peter began to speak to them: "I truly understand that God shows no partiality, but in every nation anyone who fears him and does what is right is acceptable to him. You know the message he sent to the people of Israel, preaching peace by Jesus Christ–he is Lord of all'" (Acts 10:34–37). Amazement as a reaction is also a feature of Luke–Acts: Matthew (7); Mark (4); Luke (13); John (6); Acts (5).

(V. 19)

The only two other occurrences of the word 'treasured' illustrate the range of meaning rather well: (i) 'Neither is new wine put into old wineskins; otherwise, the skins burst, and the wine is spilled, and the skins are destroyed; but new wine is put into fresh wineskins, and so both are *preserved*' (Matthew 9:17); (ii) 'for Herod feared John, knowing that he was a righteous and holy man, and he *protected* him. When he heard him, he was greatly perplexed; and yet he liked to listen to him' (Mark 6:20).

In the New Testament, the other word 'pondered' is limited to Luke-Acts (Luke 2:19; 14:31; Acts 4:15; 17:18; 18:27; 20:14). The meaning ranges from the literal (to take with) to the metaphorical (to consider, to discuss). Heart also has a certain prominence in Luke–Acts: Matthew (16); Mark (11); Luke (22); John (7); Acts (20).

(V. 20)

To glorify has a limited frequency in Luke–Acts, but of course it is extensively used in John's Gospel: Matthew (4); Mark (1); Luke (9); John

(23); Acts (5). The gospel ends with something very like this: 'and they were continually in the temple blessing God' (Luke 24:53). Praising, even if not that common, is special to Luke–Acts: Matthew (0); Mark (0); Luke (3); John (0); Acts (3). 'Seen and heard' make an interesting combination. Cf. 'And he answered them, "Go and tell John what you have seen and heard: the blind receive their sight, the lame walk, the lepers are cleansed, the deaf hear, the dead are raised, the poor have good news brought to them"' (Luke 7:22). 'Then he said, "The God of our ancestors has chosen you to know his will, to see the Righteous One and to hear his own voice; for you will be his witness to all the world of what you have seen and heard. And now why do you delay? Get up, be baptised, and have your sins washed away, calling on his name"' (Acts 22:14–16).

Pointers for prayer

a) This was no ordinary child. It is the birth of the Son of God. In order to take in the implications of that we can do well to recall Meister Eckhart's reflection and ask ourselves how the birth of Jesus takes place in us: *What good is it to me if the eternal birth of the divine Son takes place unceasingly but does not take place within myself? And what good is it to me if Mary is full of grace and if I am not also full of grace?*

b) The shepherds were both frightened and thrilled. Good news can sometimes be terrifying. Pregnancy and the birth of a child can give rise to both feelings. Hopefully the joy and wonder at new life outweigh the fear and apprehension. What has been your experience?

Prayer

Today, O God of light, your loving kindness dawns, your tender compassion breaks upon us, for in our Saviour, born of human flesh, you reveal your gracious gift of our birth to life eternal.

Fill us with the wonder of this holy day: let us treasure in our hearts what we have been told, that our lives may proclaim your great and gentle mercy.

We make our prayer through Jesus Christ, your Word made flesh, who lives and reigns with you in the unity of the Holy Spirit, in the splendour of eternal light, for ever and ever. Amen.

🍃 Second Reading 🍃

Tit 3:3 *For we ourselves were once foolish, disobedient, led astray, slaves to various passions and pleasures, passing our days in malice and envy, despicable, hating one another.* 4 But when the goodness and loving kindness (*philanthrōpia*) of God our Saviour appeared, 5 he saved us, not because of any works of righteousness that we had done, but according to his mercy, through the water of rebirth and renewal by the Holy Spirit. 6 This Spirit he poured out on us richly through Jesus Christ our Saviour, 7 so that, having been justified by his grace, we might become heirs according to the hope of eternal life. 8 *The saying is sure.*

Initial observations

There are three emphases which make this an attractive reading for Christmas: (i) the loving kindness of God (lit. God's *philanthropy*); (ii) all is gift and grace; (iii) through the Holy Spirit, we too become the sons and daughters of God, co-heirs with Christ.

Kind of writing

The Pastorals present themselves as personal letters from Paul to significant companions. In reality, they are written to communities (in Asia Minor) to bring Pauline doctrine into a later context, responding to new pastoral demands. They preserve, however, the letter structure, as in the case of Titus:

1:1–4 Salutation
1:5–3:11 *Body of the letter*
3:12–15 Travels, greetings, blessing
The body of the letter:
1:5–9 Elders

1:10–16 Warnings
2:1–10 The Christian household
2:11–15 Appearance of Christ
3:1–11 **To the whole church**

The layout of the final chapter is clear:

Practical instruction: vv. 1–2
Theological support: vv. 3–8a
Direct encouragement: vv. 8b–11

The omitted verses 3 and 8 of the central section are included for completeness. Our reading is one of the 'faithful' sayings found in the Pastorals: 1 Timothy 1:15; 3:1; 4:9; 2 Timothy 2:11; and here in Titus 3:8.

Origin of the reading

The writer(s) of the Pastorals were facing a variety of threats at the start of the second century. In response, it is true that there is some domestication of the radical Paul but there is more to it than that.

As noted before, the letters also represent a development of Pauline doctrine in several directions: (i) spirits, angels and the Holy Spirit; (ii) the church as the household of God, with great regard for the inspired Jewish Scriptures. The tension towards the end found in Paul is abandoned – there will still be a second coming, but it is in the very indefinite future. As for date and place, mostly likely it comes from Asia Minor, around the year 100.

Related passages

For the *grace* of *God* has *appeared*, bringing *salvation* to all *people*. (Titus 2:11)

This passage from Ephesians is remarkably similar to our reading.

All of us once lived among them in the passions of our flesh, following the desires of flesh and senses, and we were by nature children of wrath, like everyone else. But God, who is rich in mercy, out of the great love with which he loved us even when we were dead through our trespasses, made us alive together with Christ – by grace you have been saved – and raised us up with him and seated us with him in the heavenly places in Christ Jesus, so that in the ages to come he might show the immeasurable riches of his grace in kindness towards us in Christ Jesus. (Ephesians 2:3–7)

It is not because of your righteousness or the uprightness of your heart that you are going in to occupy their land; but because of the wickedness of these nations the LORD your God is dispossessing them before you, in order to fulfil the promise that the LORD made on oath to your ancestors, to Abraham, to Isaac, and to Jacob. (Deuteronomy 9:5)

Brief commentary

(V. 4)
The goodness of God is a genuinely Pauline expression (e.g. Romans 2:4; 3:12; 11:22). God's 'philanthropy' is rarer, being found only in Acts 28:2. The New Jerusalem Bible gets it right: the kindness and *love* of God our Saviour for *humanity*. To appear and appearance are typical of the vocabulary of later generations. Saviour – oddly rare in the Gospels and in Paul – is also an expression of later Christianity.

(V. 5a)
This verse is perhaps the clearest statement in all the Bible that salvation is wholly the initiative of God. The sentiment is not anti-Jewish because ancient Israelites/Jews were well aware of their status as the *elect* (see Deuteronomy 9:5 above). Neither is it a restatement of Paul – who contrasts grace *not with works of righteousness* but with the *ritual law* (dietary laws etc.). Neither is it saying that works don't matter: it is simply affirming that our relationship with God is initiated and sustained by God's grace alone.

(Vv. 5b–6)
Christians enter this grace through (i) baptism and the gift of the Spirit (ii) renewal (a word confined to Christian usage) and (iii) Jesus Christ

our Saviour. For this writer, Saviour refers first to God the Father as giver and then to Jesus as the mediator. The Spirit receives less emphasis in the Pastorals, perhaps reflecting the settling down (institutionalisation) of The Way.

(V. 7)

As the final verse in the lectionary excerpt, these words bring out the goal of the coming of Christ: that we might be heirs with him. Two Pauline themes are reflected here: justification by grace and becoming sons and daughters of God.

Pointers for prayer

a) In the secular celebration of Christmas, the giving of gifts is the defining action. Relationship and love, wonder and gratitude all come into play – and not only in our human interconnectedness, but also in God's love affair with humanity.

b) Christmas is a time of rest and refreshment. This is good – and yet, it would be a pity not to rest in God too and experience refreshment in the faith. What shall *I* do to bring that about?

Prayer

Abba, father and creator, we stand before you, in awe and thankfulness.

As we experience your gracious 'philanthropy', help us to become more and more like you, loving as we have been loved. Thus, may we become ever more truly your sons and daughters. Through Christ our Lord. Amen.

🍃 First Reading 🍃

Is 62:11 Look, the LORD announces to the entire earth:
    'Say to Daughter Zion,
    'Look, your deliverer comes!
    Look, his reward is with him
    and his reward goes before him!'
12   They will be called, 'The Holy People,

the Ones Protected by the LORD'.
You will be called, 'Sought After,
City Not Abandoned'.

Initial observations

The questions being addressed by Third Isaiah have a contemporary ring to them: Could they really believe God had forgiven them? In the light of recent experience, could they count on God's continued protection? Who could possibly be the leader of the community? Even more importantly, how could they live so that they might avoid repeating the sins and errors which brought on them the calamity of the Exile in Babylon? All this is not so obvious in the short excerpt chosen for the dawn Mass of Christmas Day. Nevertheless, v.11 reflects the idea that salvation is *not yet* a present reality while v. 12 expresses the feelings still remembered from the Exile – a city *forsaken*.

None of this should take away from the real joy of the reading; but just as there is no cheap grace, there is likewise no cheap joy.

Kind of writing

All of Isaiah 62 is poetry, of course, and these few verses derive their power from the poetry. The typical parallelism is not exact, but the 'uneasy synonymity' (R. Alter) has undoubted energy.

Origin of the reading

As just noted, this reading comes from Third Isaiah, that is, from the final chapters 56–66. The exiles have returned after the fall of Babylon in 539 and the victory of Cyrus. However, not all have returned, reconstruction is difficult and there is conflict between two groups in the community. The centrepiece of the writing is chapters 60–62, with five units before (56:1–8; 56:9–57:13; 57:14–21; 58; 59) and five units after (63:1–6; 63:7–64:2; 65; 66:1–16; 66:17–24).

Related Passages

(i) Daughter Zion: this term appears twenty–six times in the Old Testament, sometimes in parallel with 'daughter Jerusalem'. It appears in two contexts: disaster and redemption. As an example, reference may be made to the book of Lamentations (Lamentations 1:6; 2:1, 4, 8, 10, 13, 18; 4:22), and there is a striking example in Jeremiah: *For I heard a cry as of a woman in labour, anguish as of one bringing forth her first child, the cry of daughter Zion gasping for breath, stretching out her hands, 'Woe is me! I am fainting before killers!'* (Jeremiah 4:31).

In these contexts, the language conveys both vulnerability and defilement. In the more positive settings, the language can be quite upbeat. Here is an example, later cited in the New Testament: *Rejoice greatly, O daughter Zion! Shout aloud, O daughter Jerusalem! Lo, your king comes to you; triumphant and victorious is he, humble and riding on a donkey, on a colt, the foal of a donkey* (Zechariah 9:9; see Matthew 21:5; John 12:15). This refers to a future restoration and the joy that it will bring. The beginnings of such a positive note are found already in Isaiah 52: *Shake yourself from the dust, rise up, O captive Jerusalem; loose the bonds from your neck, O captive daughter Zion!* (Isaiah 52:2).

(ii) Marriage symbolism for God's faithfulness to Israel. At this stage, all of Isaiah 62 should really be read.

(iii) Redeemed of the Lord: in using this expression, Third Isaiah picks up a major theme of Deutero-Isaiah 40–55 (43:1; 44:22–23; 48:20; 52:9). For Second Isaiah, this redemption had already begun in the exile and is to be completed by the return of the deportees. God is also called a redeemer in these passages: Isaiah 41:14; 43:14; 44:6; 47:4; 48:17; 49:7, 26; 54:5, 8). In Third Isaiah, God is called redeemer three times (Isaiah 59:20; 60:16; 63:16).

Brief commentary

(V. 11)

The word used for proclaim means to cause to hear (cf. the *Shema Yisrael*) and is found frequently in Isaiah 40–66 (Isaiah 41:22, 26; 42:2, 9; 43:9,

12; 44:8; 45:21; 48:3, 5–6, 20; 52:7; 58:4; 62:11). This proclamation is to the whole world – a little exaggeration in the context – but not untypical of Isaiah 40–66 (Isaiah 42:10; 43:6; 48:20; 49:6; 62:11). Recompense is a positive statement of the earlier expression: 'Speak tenderly to Jerusalem, and cry to her that she has served her term, that her penalty is paid, that she has received from the Lord's hand double for all her sins' (Isaiah 40:2).

(V. 12)

The Holy People: the force of this 'title' becomes apparent when one reads Leviticus 17–26, the so-called Holiness Code. In that portion of the book, Israel is repeatedly called to be holy as YWHW is holy (e.g., 19:2; 20:7–8, 26; 21:8, 23; 22:9, 16, 33). This holiness of the people challenges another tradition that would confine holiness to the sanctuary. In this view, the holiness of the people is achieved both through ritual and social practices. One text may serve to illustrate: 'Consecrate yourselves therefore, and be holy; for I am the Lord your God. Keep my statutes, and observe them; I am the Lord; I sanctify you' (Leviticus 20:7–8). Remote as Leviticus may seem, it is part of the foundation of the Second Vatican Council's teaching on the Church as the People of God. The import of 'sought out' can best be felt by reading Song of Songs 3:1–2, 5:5. The other metaphors – redeemed and not forsaken – were explored a little above. It becomes evident that this apparently slight reading is full of resonance and is really very appropriate for the feast of Christmas.

Pointers for prayer

a) 'Salvation' is one of those words we use in Church circles. It might be useful to go back to any experience of your own where you felt 'saved'. Examples could be coming through a health crisis, restoring a fractured relationship, emerging from bereavement or depression. These experiences can lead to an understanding of salvation in Christ: freedom from fear of death, purpose in life, forgiveness of sins.

b) When we reflect on the Church, it is good to be reminded

that it is first and foremost the people of God, even 'the holy people' of God. Through these difficult times, there is great life and hope in the continued fidelity and extraordinary commitment of the 'ordinary' faithful. Time for prayer of praise and thanks!

Prayer

Loving shepherd of the sheep, always seeking the lost and strayed, today, let us hear again your good news of salvation; touch our hearts that we may know afresh your love for us in Jesus Christ, your Son, who lives and reigns with you in the unity of the Holy Spirit, in the splendour of eternal light. God for ever and ever. Amen

Themes across the readings

The dawn Mass (perhaps rarely celebrated) has much shorter readings very suitable for the time of day: light, kindness, love, astonishment, contemplation, thanksgiving. Amen.

Chapter 8

Christmas Day Mass ABC

Thought for the day

There is ongoing research into how certain animals manage to communicate, establishing some commonality with human beings. Such investigation makes it clear, however, that language, in its complexity and depth, is distinctively human, a mark of who we are. When we speak, something deeply personal goes out from us, in a manner of speaking. Words are personal, mysterious, powerful (cf. *a soft tongue can break a bone*. Proverbs 25:15). God, too, discloses himself: in the 'word' of creation, in the words of the prophets and, now, in the Word made flesh, God's deepest and most personal disclosure. We give thanks for God's 'eloquence' in Jesus of Nazareth, as we mark his birth.

Prayer

You have spoken, O God, shattered our deafness, and we can hear you in one like ourselves. Let celebrated the feast, then, in love and great joy.

🌿 Gospel 🌿

Jn 1:1 In the beginning was the Word, and the Word was with God, and the Word was God. ² He was in the beginning with God. ³ All things came into being through him, and without him not one thing came into being. What has come into being ⁴ in him was life, and the life was the light of all people. ⁵ The light shines in the darkness, and the darkness did not overcome it.

⁶ There was a man sent from God, whose name was John. ⁷ He came as a witness to testify to the light, so that all might believe through him. ⁸ He himself was not the light, but he came to testify to the light. ⁹ The true light, which enlightens everyone, was coming into the world.

¹⁰ He was in the world, and the world came into being through him; yet the world did not know him. ¹¹ He came to what was his own, and his own people did not accept him. ¹² But to all who received him, who believed in his name, he gave power to become children of God, ¹³ who were born, not of blood or of the will of the flesh or of the will of man, but of God.

¹⁴ And the Word became flesh and lived among us, and we have seen his glory, the glory as of a father's only son, full of grace and truth. ¹⁵ (John testified to him and cried out, 'This was he of whom I said, "He who comes after me ranks ahead of me because he was before me."') ¹⁶ From his fullness we have all received, grace upon grace. ¹⁷ The law indeed was given through Moses; grace and truth came through Jesus Christ. ¹⁸ No one has ever seen God. It is God the only Son, who is close to the Father's heart, who has made him known.

Initial observations

All four gospels open with a key to understanding Jesus' deep identity before the story of the ministry proper begins. Even Mark 1:1 fulfils this function: *The beginning of the good news of Jesus Christ, the Son of God.* The writer of the Fourth Gospel takes up the challenge of the word 'beginning' and fills it with deeper meaning for all those born again.

Kind of writing

These verses adapt an early Jewish Christian hymn to Wisdom, which may have looked something like this:

1   In the beginning was Wisdom
        and Wisdom was with God

and God (divine) was Wisdom [read: Wisdom was divine]
2 The same (she) was in the beginning with God
3a All things through her became
4 What became in her was life
And the life was the light of men
5 And the light in the darkness shines
And the darkness did not extinguish it
10 In the world she was
and the world through her became
And the world did not know her.
11 Unto her own she came,
And her own did not receive her.
12a But as many as received her,
12b She gave them authority
children of God to become
14a/b And Wisdom tabernacled among us.

It is likely that the final editor (i) changed the language from 'wisdom' to 'word' and (ii) inserted the prose additions putting John the Baptist firmly in his theological place (thus interrupting the poetry). (iii) Before that again, someone added elements in vv. 16–18 which have a Pauline feel to them. Thus, there is quite a bit of history behind the present text. The change from wisdom to word entailed the loss of the feminine imagery, alas. It brought with it the advantage that logos serves to unite important themes: creation (by word), prophecy (word), gospel (the word) and incarnation in the person of Jesus (the word made flesh). It mirrors the shift from Jesus in his words proclaiming the kingdom, to the early Christians proclaiming Jesus as the Word and as king, God's revelation in a human person.

Scholars have also found a concentric pattern across this carefully constructed text. D gives the benefits of faith in the Word made flesh.

A. (1–5) God, creation, humans
B. (6–8) John the Baptist
C. (9–11) The light; his rejection
D. (12–13) Faith in the Word

C'.   (14) The word; his rejection
B'.   (15) John the Baptist
A'.   (16–18) God, creation, humans.

NB: Note the error in the Jerusalem Bible version in the lectionary. In vv. 12–13, 'who *was* born' ought to read 'who *were* born'. The difference is considerable.

Old Testament background

Read Proverbs 8:22–31.

Divine wisdom had long served as one of the most important bridge concepts for a Judaism seeking to present itself intelligibly and appealingly within the context of the wider religious and philosophical thought of the time. Within Judaism itself, Wisdom (along with Spirit and Word) was one important way of speaking of God in his creative, revelatory, and redemptive immanence (Proverbs, Sirach, Wisdom, Philo of Alexandria). At the same time, the language was able to negotiate the 'beyond' of God. Judaism's (later) distinctive claim was that this wisdom was now embodied in the Torah (Sirach 24:23; Baruch 4:1). The language of 'word' (*logos*) was used by the Stoic philosophers to express the presence of God penetrating all that is (cf. Acts 17). Both the Hebrew and the Greek traditions were negotiating, so to speak, the transcendence and the immanence of God. Good examples of this kind of writing can be found in Proverbs 8 and Wisdom 7. Genesis 1:1–2:4a is also very much in the mind of the writer.

New Testament foreground

Here we notice in bullet point form the resonance of this language throughout the Fourth Gospel:

* *New creation* across the Fourth Gospel – beginning, finished, first day of the week (John 1; 20; 21). Cf. Genesis 1:1–2:4a.
* *Life* – the Lazarus story – I am the Resurrection and the Life (John 11).
* *Light* – the Blind Man – I am the Light of the world (John 9).
* *The Baptist* – important early on in the gospel (John 1–3).
* *Not know him* – the rejection by most Jews (John 5 and 18–19).

- *Children and being born* – Nicodemus (John 3).
- *Flesh* – cf. Thomas and Tiberias (John 20–21).
- *Glory* – throughout this gospel, glory and glorification are used to refer to the revelation of God's deep self in the single event of the death and resurrection of Jesus.
- *Father's only Son* – see the long discourses in John 13–17 which express and 'unpack' the relationship.
- *Truth* – Pilate and often elsewhere; I am the truth (John 19).
- *'He was before me '* – Before Abraham was, I Am' (John 8:58 – but throughout in the well-known I am pronouncements in this gospel).
- *Made him known* – revealed through actions and speech, seen especially in the long meditations in the Fourth Gospel (most likely not the words of the historical Jesus, but late first-century meditations).

St Paul

For it is the God who said, 'Let light shine out of darkness', who has shone in our hearts to give the light of the knowledge of the glory of God in the face of Jesus Christ. (2 Corinthians 4:6)

Brief commentary

(V. 1)
The context is the original creation and the new creation in Christ. The Word expresses and articulates the deep being of God.

(V. 2)
The New Testament writers became aware quite early of Jesus' identity with God. This is one of strongest statements.

(V. 3)
Cf. Colossians 1:15–20 and Ephesians 1:3–14.

(V. 4)
The images of light and life recur throughout this gospel.

(V. 5)
The writer states the victory of Jesus over death before coming to the tragic rejection of the Word by God's first chosen people.

(Vv. 6–9)
Anxiety about John makes the writer clarify the relationship with Jesus. This is most likely on account of the continued existence of disciples of John the Baptist, who might claim a certain superiority. Cf. *Mandaeans* of today.

(Vv. 10–11)
Paradoxical and tragic.

(Vv. 12–13)
The literary and theological anticipation of the effects of incarnation may be seen here.

(V. 14)
An echo of both wisdom and God's presence (*shekinah*) in the ark of the covenant; at the time, highly paradoxical because of the juxtaposition of word (*logos*) and flesh (*sarx*). 'Grace and truth' are the same as 'love and faithfulness,' God's covenant qualities in the Old Testament, coming to personal expression in the person of Jesus of Nazareth.

(V. 15)
Prose interruption again to 'locate' John the Baptist.

(V. 16)
God's prodigal gift of love in the Son.

(V. 17)
The contrast of Law and grace sounds Pauline at this point.

(V. 18)
Cf. 1 John 4:12. 'Made him known' = lit. to relate in detail, to expound or, perhaps, to tell the story.

Pointers for prayer

a) 'In the beginning' takes me back to my own new creation in Christ – back to significant moments – perhaps even to a single moment which stands out as the beginning of my own belonging in Christ. A prayer of praise.

b) Life – what makes me alive, taking hold of my imagination and energy? How is my life in Christ? Prayer of gratitude.

c) Light – a fabulous imagery. It may be that some particular land or seascape stands out in my memory as having an especially beautiful light. Prayer of enlightenment.

d) The dark side of refusal and rejection – In my life I probably have said both yes and no to grace. Where am I now in my life? Prayer of pilgrimage.

e) Wisdom was God's presence – a feminine presence, because (to use biblical language) just as a man is 'incomplete' without the love and companionship of a woman, the human person needs to be complemented by God's wisdom.

f) The power of language in my experience as an entry point to appreciating the Word made flesh. What word am I hearing especially today?

Prayer

We praise you, gracious God, for the glad tidings of peace, the good news of salvation: your Word became flesh and we have seen his glory. Let the radiance of that glory enlighten the lives of those who celebrate his birth.

Reveal to all the world the light no darkness can extinguish, our Lord Jesus Christ, who lives and reigns with you in the unity of the Holy Spirit, in the splendour of eternal light, God for ever and ever. Amen.

🌿 Second Reading 🌿

Heb 1:1 Long ago God spoke to our ancestors in many and various ways by the prophets, [2] but in these last days he has spoken to us by a Son, whom he appointed heir of all things, through whom he also created the worlds. [3] He is the reflection (*apaugasma*) of God's glory and the exact imprint (*charactēr*) of God's very being (*hypostasis*), and he sustains all things by his powerful word. When he had made purification for sins, he sat down at the right hand of the Majesty on high, [4] having become as much superior to angels as the name he has inherited is more excellent than theirs.

⁵ For to which of the angels did God ever say, 'You are my Son; today I have begotten you'? Or again, 'I will be his Father, and he will be my Son'? ⁶ And again, when he brings the firstborn into the world, he says, 'Let all God's angels worship him.'

Initial observations

The stately opening of Hebrews, sonorous even in English, makes this an ideal reading for Christmas Day – poetic and dignified, mysterious and intriguing. Even here, however, something of the puzzle of Hebrews come to the fore. Who wrote it? To whom? When? In what circumstances? Much remains speculative, although the implied context can be inferred (see below). Today, scholars would claim this is not a letter but a homily in which the author wants to show that Jesus' death *both* fulfils *and* abolishes the Temple service. This deep understanding of Jesus' death and resurrection is built upon the foundation of Jesus as the final and complete disclosure of God (Son, heir, 'reflection' and 'imprint').

Kind of writing

This early Christian homily is written in the best Greek of the NT, using all the techniques of ancient rhetoric, 'the art of speaking well'. In particular, we note the sustained use of comparison (*synkrisis*): prophets, angels, Moses, Aaron and the temple cult. Our reading is part of the introduction to the opening section, 1:1–4; 1:5–4:13. The four opening verses form an introduction (*exordium*) while vv. 5–6 initiate the first comparison with the angels. As an *exordium*, the opening verses attract the attention and good will of the audience and lay out the themes to be treated in the course of the whole homily.

Origin of the reading

A careful reading of the letter allows a tentative reconstruction of the context of writing. (i) The community, after initial conversion and enthusiasm, encountered considerable opposition from the surrounding culture. (ii) Within the group, some fell away because of the gap between Christian claims and reality. (iii) The many exhortations reveal the anxiety of the author that more will fall away. (iv) The teaching that 'Jesus can help us because he is like us' reveals the context of suffering and trials and a sense of alienation. The author addresses the context in two ways: theology (really Christology) and much practical exhortation/ *paraenesis*. Our verses focus on the Christology of Hebrews.

Related passages

Many New Testament passages echo the high Christology of Hebrews.

> All things came into being through him, and without him not one thing came into being. (John 1:3)

> For from him and through him and to him are all things. To him be the glory forever. Amen. (Romans 11:36)

> Indeed, even though there may be so-called gods in heaven or on earth – as in fact there are many gods and many lords – yet for us there is one God, the Father, from whom are all things and for whom we exist, and one Lord, Jesus Christ, through whom are all things and through whom we exist. (1 Corinthians 8:5–6)

> He is the image of the invisible God, the firstborn of all creation; for in him all things in heaven and on earth were created, things visible and invisible, whether thrones or dominions or rulers or powers – all things have been created through him and for him. (Colossians 1:15–16)

> For it is the God who said, 'Let light shine out of darkness,' who has shone in our hearts to give the light of the knowledge of the glory of God in the face of Jesus Christ. (2 Corinthians 4:6)

Brief commentary

(V. 1)

Already the tone of comparison is established, within an affirmation of continuity (*our* ancestors ... *but*).

(V. 2)

Notice how comprehensive the claims are: the present (Son), the end/ future (heir), the beginning/past (creation). As believers, we become accustomed to such claims but, as Raymond Brown remarked many years ago, these *are* extraordinary claims about a Galilean peasant prophet who was put to death ignominiously by the Romans.

(V. 3a)

The imagery here (given in Greek above) comes not only from the Wisdom tradition of the Bible but also from philosophical speculation, in the works of Philo of Alexandria, for example.

(V. 3b)

Thus the writer announces the main argument of Hebrews: Jesus fulfils, transcends and abolishes the Temple priesthood. The challenge is acute because the *historical* Jesus was a prophet and a layman, not a priest.

(V. 4)

The final sentence of the introduction acts as a bridge to the next section, the comparison with the angels.

(V. 5)

The rhetorical questions make use of Psalm 2, found elsewhere (Acts 13:23; Hebrews 5:5). At the time, Psalm 2 was widely read in a messianic manner.

(V. 6)

The verse cited is from the Septuagint of Deuteronomy 32:43: *Be glad, O nations, with his people, and let all the angels of God prevail* (= *worship* in Hebrews) *for him.*

Pointers for prayer

a) Can I go back to my own times of 'disclosure', when I was aware of God's word to me in a special way?

a) Christians don't just say things *about* Jesus; instead, we encounter him as God's living word in our world. Building on such personal experience, we become more and more aware of the depth and mystery of the identity of Jesus.

Prayer

In your words to us, O God, you have disclosed yourself and guided our steps. In the Word made flesh, you have done something even more wonderful: we see the very imprint of your being, as you speak to us from within our fractured humanity. Help us to come to you through Jesus, our Lord and brother, who can help us because he is one of us and knows our lives from the inside out. Through Christ our Lord. Amen.

🍃 First Reading 🍃

Is 52:7 How delightful it is to see approaching over the mountains
the feet of a messenger who announces peace,
a messenger who brings good news, who announces deliverance,
who says to Zion, 'Your God reigns!'

8 Listen, your watchmen shout;
in unison they shout for joy,
for they see with their very own eyes
the LORD's return to Zion.

9 In unison give a joyful shout,
O ruins of Jerusalem!
For the LORD consoles his people;
he protects Jerusalem.

10 The LORD reveals his royal power
in the sight of all the nations;
the entire earth sees
our God deliver.

Initial observations

This reading is very suitable for the third Mass of Christmas Day. It has an energetic, uplifting tone and the words touch on the important themes of the feast (peace, good news, salvation, joy, and so forth).

Kind of writing

Once again, this is poetry, showing the usual marks of parallelism. Part of the imagery includes reference to the Holy City (Zion, Jerusalem, sentinels on the look-out). We see also the language of proclamation (announces, brings good news), the language of response (sing, joy, singing) and the language of God's gifts (peace, good news, salvation, return, comforted, redeemed, holy arm, salvation of our God). The pleasure of biblical parallelism can be noted here:

> 7 who brings good news, who announces salvation, who says to Zion, 'Your God reigns.' 8 Listen! Your sentinels lift up their voices, together they sing for joy; 9 for the Lord has comforted his people, he has redeemed Jerusalem. (Isaiah 52:7)

It is said once more that God will be returning with them, because in Exile God was with them all along. It shares that vision with Isaiah 40:3–5 (see below). It may well be that the exhilaration found here comes from some who returned early and felt the relief and joy.

Origin of the reading

As we have seen regularly in Advent, Isaiah is almost a fifth gospel for early Christianity, so widely was it used. It does come from a difficult time, that is, during the Babylonian Exile (587–539 BC). The whole section runs from our v. 7 as far as v. 12. It is, in effect, a prophecy of restoration, offering the exiles an ecstatic vision of hope and renewal. It comes as a response to v. 6, which reads: *Therefore my people shall know my name; therefore in that day they shall know that it is I who speak; here am I* (Isaiah 52:6).

Related passages

A voice cries out: 'In the wilderness prepare the way of the Lord, make straight in the desert a highway for our God. Every valley shall be lifted up, and every mountain and hill be made low; the uneven ground shall become level, and the rough places a plain. Then the glory of the Lord shall be revealed, and all people shall see it together, for the mouth of the Lord has spoken.' (Isaiah 40:3–5)

Then the watcher called out: 'Upon a watchtower I stand, O Lord, continually by day, and at my post I am stationed throughout the night'. (Isaiah 21:8)

Lift up your heads, O gates! and be lifted up, O ancient doors! that the King of glory may come in. Who is the King of glory? The Lord, strong and mighty, the Lord, mighty in battle. Lift up your heads, O gates! and be lifted up, O ancient doors! that the King of glory may come in. Who is this King of glory? The Lord of hosts, he is the King of glory. (Psalms 24:7–10) Cf. Psalm 47:1–9.

Brief commentary

(V. 7)

In a striking rhetorical figure, even the (presumably humble, even pedestrian!) feet of the messengers are praised for their beauty! The message is peace, *shalom*, i.e. a gift of wholeness, affecting the whole person within a network of relationships. It includes the healing of the wound of the Exile for one and for all.

The imagery echoes that of a victorious monarch returning. 'Bringing good news' is a verb in the Hebrew Bible ('goodnewsing', or something like that – in any event, an action). The New Testament noun gospel or good news comes precisely from Isaiah. The Psalms often speak of universal salvation (Psalms 96:10; 97:1; 99:1).

(V. 8)

This verse voices the longing of those in the city who are on the alert for God's return. There is a contrast with Isaiah 21:8, where one sentinel is alone. Here, they are united in their reaction to the 'second exodus' of God's return to Zion.

(V. 9)

This captures the context of the Exile – the ruin of Jerusalem. God comforts by means of redemption or salvation. Poetically, it is the very stones of Jerusalem that cry out.

(V. 10)

The arm is a standard image in the Bible for the power of God, and to bare the arm is to let God's power be seen or felt. In the eyes of the poet, this is an international event, taking place in sight of all the nations, all the ends of the earth. See Psalm 98.

Pointers for prayer

a) To hear good news is a wonderful thing. Go back to some experience of your own which brought you particular delight. When did you first come to appreciate the good news of the Kingdom of God?

b) Peace is also a wonderful word, particularly in the Bible, where it means health, prosperity, good relationships. Thank God for the well-being you enjoy!

c) The joy that Christmas brings comes to delightful expression in today's first reading. Let the happiness of the feast touch your own heart today, so that you are renewed in Christ and have cause for singing.

d) Salvation for all is the great message of Christmas: this is our God and we extol him. *No one has ever seen God. It is God the only Son, who is close to the Father's heart, who has made him known* (John 1:18). Let us rejoice and be glad!

Prayer

God, so close to us that we can hardly believe it, draw us into the circle of your love so that our celebration of the birth of Christ will bring us new life and true joy as we continue on the way of your salvation.
Through Christ our Lord. Amen.

Themes across the readings

The readings for the day Mass invite us to lift our sights: the birth of Jesus *matters* for all humanity, for the world as a whole and even for the cosmos. In him, creation comes to fulfilment and in him creation itself is made new. It is a grand vision – yet rooted in history, in the individual, concrete life of Jesus of Nazareth. 'Indeed, from his fullness we have, all of us, received.'

Chapter 9

Feast of the Holy Family B

For this feast, there are alternatives for the first and second readings. Accordingly, the notes will offer comments on the full range of texts, indicating the options by First Reading (1), First Reading (2) and so forth.

Thought for the day

Our Gospel today describes two very old people – Simeon and Anna – who are very attractive in their old age. They have lived prayerful lives of faith and, in particular, of hope and expectation. Being wise, they are people of discernment and they recognise the moment of grace, the coming of the Messiah. Wouldn't it be wonderful to be like them in old age? The secret is to be now what we hope to be then. If we wish to be serene, wise, discerning, full of faith – then now is the time: *See, now is the acceptable time; see, now is the day of salvation!* (2 Corinthians 6:2).

Prayer

Abba, Father, God of all time, you call us to become your children. Send your Holy Spirit into our hearts that we may live our faith serenely in the present moment and give us grace to recognise the time of your appearing. Through Christ our Lord. Amen.

 Gospel

Lk 2:22 When the time came for their purification according to the law of Moses, the parents of Jesus brought him up to Jerusalem to present him to the Lord [23] (as it is written in the law of the Lord, 'Every firstborn male shall be designated as holy to the Lord'), [24] and they offered a sacrifice according to what is stated in the law of the Lord, 'a pair of turtledoves or two young pigeons'.

[25] Now there was a man in Jerusalem whose name was Simeon; this man was righteous and devout, looking forward to the consolation of Israel, and the Holy Spirit rested on him. [26] It had been revealed to him by the Holy Spirit that he would not see death before he had seen the Lord's Messiah. [27] Guided by the Spirit, Simeon came into the temple; and when the parents brought in the child Jesus, to do for him what was customary under the law, [28] Simeon took him in his arms and praised God, saying,

[29] 'Master, now you are dismissing your servant in peace, according to your word; [30] for my eyes have seen your salvation, [31] which you have prepared in the presence of all peoples, [32] a light for revelation to the Gentiles and for glory to your people Israel.'

[33] And the child's father and mother were amazed at what was being said about him. [34] Then Simeon blessed them and said to his mother Mary, 'This child is destined for the falling and the rising of many in Israel, and to be a sign that will be opposed [35] so that the inner thoughts of many will be revealed – and a sword will pierce your own soul too.'

[36] There was also a prophet, Anna the daughter of Phanuel, of the tribe of Asher. She was of a great age, having lived with her husband seven years after her marriage, [37] then as a widow to the age of eighty-four. She never left the temple but worshipped there with fasting and prayer night and day. [38] At that moment she came, and began to praise God and to speak about the child to all who were looking for the redemption of Jerusalem.

[39] When they had finished everything required by the law of the Lord, they returned to Galilee, to their own town of Nazareth. [40] The child grew and became strong, filled with wisdom; and the favour of God was upon him.

Initial observations

This story is also read for the Presentation (2 February), which used to be called the Purification, a word is still mentioned at the very start of the reading. The change of name reflects perhaps a sensitivity around the whole idea of purification after childbirth, called churching in the not so distant past. It would not at all be helpful to dwell too much on this, but it can be understood at least from the point of view of religious anthropology.

In pre-modern cultures, contact with the sacred or the Holy rendered one 'impure' – not *morally* impure but *ritually* impure. The causes were various: contact with a corpse, any discharge of the fluids associated with procreation and, not least, childbirth itself. (a) In those days, the sacred was considered both life-giving and dangerous. You can see why. In the time before antibiotics and good hygiene, infant mortality was high and death in childbirth common. (b) The need to be 'purified' acknowledged that the sacred has been encountered in the godlike action of childbirth.

Kind of writing

Perhaps it is good to recall again that the Infancy Gospels in both Matthew and Luke are always written with four lenses: the Hebrew Bible, history, Christology and ecclesiology.

(i) *Hebrew Bible*: As we see, the anecdotes reflect Old Testament practices such as purification and circumcision. It is also the case here that Luke writes in the Greek of the Greek Old Testament, the Septuagint, creating an atmosphere of Old Testament piety and expectation in the figures of Mary and Joseph and Simeon and Anna.

(ii) *History*: The purification of Mary and circumcision of Jesus are surely historical facts, even if no other early sources confirm them.

(iii) *Christology*: The stories are written always in the light of the Resurrection.

(iv) *Ecclesiology*: The writing reflects early Christian teaching about and exploration of the identity of Jesus, using Old Testament models and themes. The patterning of stories is clear in both Matthew and Luke.

Old Testament background

Throughout your generations every male among you shall be circumcised when he is eight days old, including the slave born in your house and the one bought with your money from any foreigner who is not of your offspring. (Genesis 17:12)

On the eighth day the flesh of his foreskin shall be circumcised. (Leviticus 12:3)

Consecrate to me all the firstborn; whatever is the first to open the womb among the Israelites, of human beings and animals, is mine. (Exodus 13:2)

The first issue of the womb of all creatures, human and animal, which is offered to the LORD, shall be yours; but the firstborn of human beings you shall redeem, and the firstborn of unclean animals you shall redeem. Their redemption price, reckoned from one month of age, you shall fix at five shekels of silver, according to the shekel of the sanctuary (that is, twenty gerahs). (Numbers 18:15–16)

The LORD spoke to Moses, saying: Speak to the people of Israel, saying: If a woman conceives and bears a male child, she shall be ceremonially unclean seven days; as at the time of her menstruation, she shall be unclean. On the eighth day the flesh of his foreskin shall be circumcised. Her time of blood purification shall be thirty-three days; she shall not touch any holy thing, or come into the sanctuary, until the days of her purification are completed. If she bears a female child, she shall be unclean two weeks, as in her menstruation; her time of blood purification shall be sixty-six days. (Leviticus 12:1–5)

When the days of her purification are completed, whether for a son or for a daughter, she shall bring to the priest at the entrance of the tent of meeting a lamb in its first year for a burnt offering, and a pigeon or a turtledove for a sin offering. He shall offer it before the Lord, and make atonement on her behalf; then she shall be clean from her flow of blood. This is the law for her who bears a child, male or female. If she cannot afford a sheep, she shall take two turtledoves or two pigeons, one for a burnt offering and the other for a sin offering; and the priest shall make atonement on her behalf, and she shall be clean. (Leviticus 12:6–8)

New Testament foreground

All of Luke 1–2, in light of the comments above.

St Paul

But when the appropriate time had come, God sent out his Son, born of a woman, born under the law, to redeem those who were under the law, so that we may be adopted as sons with full rights. And because you are sons, God sent the Spirit of his Son into our hearts, who calls 'Abba! Father!' So you are no longer a slave but a son, and if you are a son, then you are also an heir through God. (Galatians 4:4–7)

Brief commentary

(Vv. 22–24)

There are three elements here: (a) purification – of the mother only, hence 'their' is odd; (b) presentation of the child (not his redemption); offering of the child to God is along the lines of Samuel. The child is not ransomed but presented (see Exodus 13).

(V. 25–32)

'Now' introduces the expected prophetic statement combining praise of God and an indication of the child's destiny. The comfort or consolation is written with Isaiah 40:1ff. in mind. The consolation of Israel is precisely in the Messiah of the Lord. Simeon models the waiting of Israel for the coming Christ. In the hymn, to dismiss means to allow to die. The particular word for salvation (sōtērion) is rare in the New Testament (Luke 2:30; 3:6; Acts 28:28; Ephesians 6:17) and almost confined to the Lucan *oeuvre*. Light is the key metaphor here. We are perhaps meant to think of Isaiah: *The Lord has bared his holy arm before the eyes of all the nations; and all the ends of the earth shall see the salvation of our God* (Isaiah 52:10). The coming of the Messiah includes glory. Cf. *I bring near my deliverance, it is not far off, and my salvation will not tarry; I will put salvation in Zion, for Israel my glory* (Isaiah 46:13). *In the Lord all the offspring of Israel shall triumph and glory* (Isaiah 45:25).

(Vv. 33–35)

There is a blessing for the parents, with a particular part addressed to Mary. Jesus' ministry will have two effects: acceptance and rejection. Behind the language of falling may lie the much-used metaphor of the stumbling block, found widely in the New Testament. The parenthesis in v. 35 here is as awkward in Greek as in English and may be editorial.

(Vv. 36–40)

Considerable emphasis is placed on Anna's advanced age and well-attested piety. 'At that very moment' is a frequent phrase in Luke: 10:21; 12:12; 13:31; 20:19; 24:33; Acts 16:18; 22:13. To praise here comprises recognition, obedience and proclamation, all done in public. V. 40 is a second 'conclusion' of sorts (cf. Luke 1:80 and 2:52). The emphasis on growth, physical, spiritual and social, goes against a constant tendency in the tradition to underplay the very real humanity of Jesus.

Pointers for prayer

a) It was a day that started without any expectation of something unusual. It turned out to be a day with a meeting they would remember for a long time. Perhaps you have had significant meetings on what you expected to be just an ordinary day?

b) Simeon gave thanks because his eyes saw the salvation God had prepared. In what ways have you experienced God's salvation in your life: an experience of being loved, or discovering a sense of purpose in life, or being touched by the wonders of creation? Give thanks for those memories.

c) Simeon also acknowledged that not all would accept the light that would shine through Jesus, and this rejection would be a cause of pain to Mary. It can be a source of pain to parents, teachers, church ministers, and all who work for others when some reject values, projects or advice that would be for their good. Even within ourselves we can be aware of division, at times being open to the light of God and at other times resisting it. Have you known the pain of that struggle? What has helped you to keep seeking the light of God in your life?

d) The final sentence speaks of Jesus as one who grew and became strong and was filled with wisdom. Recall times when you had a sense of growing up in some way. What brought that about? Think also of how you have seen growth in another person.

Prayer

O God, you cradle us at the beginning of life and embrace us at our journey's end, for you love us as your own. Bind our families together and deepen our faith, that, like the Holy Family of Nazareth, we may grow in wisdom, obedient to your word.

We ask this through Jesus Christ, your Word made flesh, who lives and reigns with you in the unity of the Holy Spirit in the splendour of eternal light, God for ever and ever. Amen.

🌿 Second Reading (1) 🌿

Col 3:12 As God's chosen ones, holy and beloved, clothe yourselves with compassion, kindness, humility, meekness, and patience. ¹³ Bear with one another and, if anyone has a complaint against another, forgive each other; just as the Lord has forgiven you, so you also must forgive. [14] Above all, clothe yourselves with love, which binds everything together in perfect harmony. [15] And let the peace of Christ rule in your hearts, to which indeed you were called in the one body. And be thankful.

[16] Let the word of Christ dwell in you richly; teach and admonish one another in all wisdom; and with gratitude in your hearts sing psalms, hymns, and spiritual songs to God. [17] And whatever you do, in word or deed, do everything in the name of the Lord Jesus, giving thanks to God the Father through him.

[18] *Wives, be subject to your husbands, as is fitting in the Lord.* [19] *Husbands, love your wives and never treat them harshly.*

[20] *Children, obey your parents in everything, for this is your acceptable duty in the Lord.* [21] *Fathers, do not provoke your children, or they may lose heart.*

Initial observations

In the Liturgical Calendar, it is recommended to use the shorter version, 3:12–17. You will see why once you read vv. 18–19, 20–21, even though these last few lines are the real reason the passage was chosen for the feast. Without mentioning family specifically, the message of harmony and forgiveness would still be of relevance today to any community or family.

Kind of writing

After an introduction (1:10–14) and a conclusion (4:7–18), the body of the letter has two parts:
    1:15–2:23 *Theology*
    3:1–4:4 *Exhortation*
    3:1–4 Summary

3:5–17 Old and new life in Christ
3:18–4:1 The Christian household
4:2–6 Conclusion and prayer

Origin of the reading

The clue for the occasion of Colossians is provided by 2:8 and its amplification in vv. 9–23 (too long to cite): *See to it that no one takes you captive through philosophy and empty deceit, according to human tradition, according to the elemental spirits of the universe, and not according to Christ* (Colossians 2:8).

From the subsequent verses, it is apparent that this 'heresy' offered a spiritual path to perfection, combining in some unclear way visions, angels, feasts, rituals, dietary laws and some kind of asceticism. The writer's assessment is both clear and negative:

> *All these regulations refer to things that perish with use; they are simply human commands and teachings. These have indeed an appearance of wisdom in promoting self-imposed piety, humility, and severe treatment of the body, but they are of no value in checking self–indulgence* (Colossians 2:22–23).

Scholars dispute the authorship, date and location of Colossians. The reason for the puzzle is that the letter is so close to Philemon and contains much Pauline vocabulary. At the same time, significant teachings are absent (for instance justification) and other teachings are taken to a new level (for example the cosmic Christ). There is also a puzzling link with Ephesians, which reads almost as a commentary on Colossians. Archaeologically, near-by Laodicea was destroyed by an earthquake in 60/61 and immediately rebuilt (at the citizens' own expense, they proudly recalled). Colossae, as far as is known, was also destroyed but was never rebuilt. Bearing in mind differences in vocabulary and unconscious differences in grammatical style (especially conjunctions and connectives, so frequent in Paul), it seems sensible to affirm the this much: The letter is a product of a post-Pauline school, written after Philemon but before Ephesians. An approximate date would be the 70s or 80s, after both the death of Paul and destruction of Colossae. All would have recognised this document as an updating of the apostle for a later time in the form of a general letter to the churches in Asia Minor. It is, therefore, the first of the Deutero-Paulines.

Related passage

> Do not get drunk with wine, for that is debauchery; but be filled with the Spirit, as you sing psalms and hymns and spiritual songs among yourselves, singing and making melody to the Lord in your hearts, giving thanks to God the Father at all times and for everything in the name of our Lord Jesus Christ. (Ephesians 5:18–20)

Brief commentary

(V. 12)
The address is familiar (cf. Romans 8:33; 1 Peter 2:9). Notice the five virtues – great for reflection.

(V. 13)
Reality is recognised: there are tensions and there is need for forgiveness. The motive is clear and comes from the teaching of Jesus (Matthew 6:14–15).

(V. 14)
Here the writer is close both to Jesus (Mark 12:28–34) and to Paul (Romans 13:8, 10; Galatians 5:14; 1 Corinthians 13).

(V. 15)
This prayer reminds Christians of the calling in Christ. Thankful in Greek is *eucharistoi*, 'grateful people'. There is a liturgical feel to the letter: Colossians 1:3; 1:12, 2:7.

(V. 16)
The first instruction is especially relevant today: the word of Christ, that is the Good News. Mutual teaching and common prayer bring it all together. Thus, taking the Word seriously is very much part of being *eucharistoi*.

(V. 17)

This is a general summary of the widest possible application: *whatever you do*. It echoes a definition of spirituality: what I do to make the Good News come alive in my life (Nivard Kinsella). Practical considerations of family life (not included in the short form) follow.

Pointers for prayer

a) Do the virtues listed speak to me in my life? It may help to be quite concrete.

b) Where in my life do I need to practise forgiveness and love?

c) How would I describe the place of the Word in my life right now?

Prayer

I pray that, according to the riches of his glory, he may grant that you may be strengthened in your inner being with power through his Spirit, and that Christ may dwell in your hearts through faith, as you are being rooted and grounded in love. I pray that you may have the power to comprehend, with all the saints, what is the breadth and length and height and depth, and to know the love of Christ that surpasses knowledge, so that you may be filled with all the fullness of God (Ephesians 3:16–19).

🌿 Second Reading (2) 🌿

Heb 11:8 By faith Abraham obeyed when he was called to set out for a place that he was to receive as an inheritance; and he set out, not knowing where he was going.

Heb 11:11 By faith he received power of procreation, even though he was too old – and Sarah herself was barren – because he considered him faithful who had promised. [12] Therefore from one person, and this one as good as dead, descendants were born, 'as many as the stars of heaven and as the innumerable grains of sand by the seashore'.

Heb 11:17 By faith Abraham, when put to the test, offered up

Isaac. He who had received the promises was ready to offer up his only son, [18] of whom he had been told, 'It is through Isaac that descendants shall be named for you.' [19] He considered the fact that God is able even to raise someone from the dead – and figuratively speaking, he did receive him back.

Initial observations

This alternative reading would go very well with the first reading from Genesis 15 and 21. The exposition of the faith of the ancestors is really an invitation to copy their good example – a perfectly good theme for the Feast of the Holy Family.

Kind of writing

(i) The Letter to the Hebrews is in five great movements or parts, with an introduction and a conclusion.

Introduction: 1:1–4
Part I: 1:5–2:8 Jesus, higher than the angels
Part II: 3:1–5:10 Jesus, trustworthy and compassionate high priest
Part III: 5:11–10:19 Jesus, the perfection of priesthood
Part IV: 11:1–12:13 Faith and endurance
Part V: 12:14–13:19 The right ways
Conclusion: 13:20–21

After the mighty theological arguments in Part III, the writer turns to example and exhortation. Part IV itself is in two parts as follows:

A. 11:1–40: The faith of the ancestors, as an example
B. 12:14–13:9: The necessary endurance, as an exhortation

Part A is the necessary doctrinal foundation for the exhortation in Part B. The emulation of faith takes the form of endurance.

(ii) The key word 'faith' runs through the entire chapter, linking each figure with the next (Hebrews 11:1, 3–9, 11, 13, 17, 20–24, 27–31, 33, 39, that is twenty-four times as a noun; the verb occurs in v.6). The opening verses (a definition of faith) are linked with the closing verses (a warning and an important link to the current generation).

Defining faith (11:1–2)
> From Cain to Enoch (11:3–5)
> The necessity of faith (11:6)
> Noah (11:7)
> *Abraham's journey* (11:8–10)
> *Abraham's offspring* (11:11–12)
> The better country (11:13–16)
> *Abraham's sacrifice* (11:17–19)
> The patriarchs (11:20–22)
> Moses (11:23–26)
> The Exodus (11:27–29)
> Joshua and Rahab (11:30–31)
> The victors (11:32–35a)
> The martyrs (11:35b–38)
> Not yet (11:39–40)

Our reading, Hebrews 11:8, 11–12, 17–19, focuses very properly on the faith of Abraham, from call and promise to the very difficult, even impossible, command to sacrifice his longed-for child, Isaac.

Origin of the reading

The implied audience of the letter can be picked up from the letter itself (the full texts are below under related passages). The title 'To the Hebrews' is secondary, although on the earliest manuscript. The text is really a very sophisticated homily in excellent Greek aimed at a mixed community of Jewish and Gentile Christians. They have been Christians for some time (Hebrews 6:1–3). Their experience of the faith has included harassment of some kind (Hebrews 10:32–35; 12:12–13). Internal challenges include hospitality (Hebrews 13:2), love of money (Hebrews 13:5), sharing what you have (Hebrews 13:16), weakening of the faith (Hebrews 5:11–12) and a decline in community belonging (Hebrews 10:24–25). Some have clearly abandoned the faith. These features bring the teaching of Hebrews very close to our own times.

On balance, Hebrews was most likely written to Roman Christians by a Roman Christian teacher from abroad.

Related passages

(i) For a picture of what was happening the community:

> Therefore we must progress beyond the elementary instructions about Christ and move on to maturity, not laying this foundation again: repentance from dead works and faith in God, teaching about baptisms, laying on of hands, resurrection of the dead and eternal judgement. And this is what we intend to do, if God permits. (Hebrews 6:1–3)

> But remember the former days when you endured a harsh conflict of suffering after you were enlightened. At times you were publicly exposed to abuse and afflictions, and at other times you came to share with others who were treated in that way. For in fact you shared the sufferings of those in prison, and you accepted the confiscation of your belongings with joy, because you knew that you certainly had a better and lasting possession. So do not throw away your confidence, because it has great reward. (Hebrews 10:32–35)

> Therefore, strengthen your listless hands and your weak knees, and make straight paths for your feet, so that what is lame may not be put out of joint but be healed. (Hebrews 12:12–13)

> Do not neglect hospitality, because through it some have entertained angels without knowing it. (Hebrews 13:2)

> Your conduct must be free from the love of money and you must be content with what you have, for he has said, 'I will never leave you and I will never abandon you.' (Hebrews 13:5)

> And do not neglect to do good and to share what you have, for God is pleased with such sacrifices. (Hebrews 13:16)

> On this topic we have much to say and it is difficult to explain, since you have become sluggish in hearing. For though you should in fact be teachers by this time, you need someone to

teach you the beginning elements of God's utterances. You have gone back to needing milk, not solid food. (Hebrews 5:11–12)

And let us take thought of how to spur one another on to love and good works, not abandoning our own meetings, as some are in the habit of doing, but encouraging each other, and even more so because you see the day drawing near. (Hebrews 10:24–25)

(ii) *The great narrative of the ancestors is found elsewhere as well: Psalm 105:8–44 or Joshua 24; Sirach 44–50; Wisdom 10.* The beginning of Sirach 44 gives the flavour.

Let us now sing the praises of famous men, our ancestors in their generations. The Lord apportioned to them great glory, his majesty from the beginning. There were those who ruled in their kingdoms, and made a name for themselves by their valour; those who gave counsel because they were intelligent; those who spoke in prophetic oracles; those who led the people by their counsels and by their knowledge of the people's lore; they were wise in their words of instruction; those who composed musical tunes, or put verses in writing; rich men endowed with resources, living peacefully in their homes – all these were honoured in their generations, and were the pride of their times. (Sirach 44:1–7)

Brief commentary

(V. 8)

This verse takes us back to Genesis 12, the foundational call to Abram (as he then was) in Genesis 12:1–3. The response of Abram is coolly reported: So Abram left, just as the LORD had told him to do (Genesis 12:4). The *book of Jubilees* offers this synthesis: *And the LORD was aware that Abraham was faithful in all of his afflictions because he tested him with his land, and with famine. And he tested him with the wealth of kings. And he tested him again with his wife, when she was taken (from him), and with circumcision. And he tested him with Ishmael and with Hagar, his maidservant, when he sent them away. And in everything in which he tested him, he was found faithful. And his soul was not impatient. And he was not slow to act because he was faithful and a lover of the* LORD (Jubilees 17:17–18).

(Vv. 11–12)

This reference to Abraham's age reinforces the emphasis on his vulnerable existence, indicating that he was not only a migrant (Hebrews 11:8–9) but near death. The memory of the remarkable birth of Isaac in Hebrews 11:11 is the basis for the conclusion that they were born from one man who was as good as dead (Hebrews 11:12a). Although God promised that his descendants would be as many as the stars of the heaven and as innumerable as the sands on the seashore (Hebrews 11:12b; Genesis 15:5–6; 22:17; 32:12), Abraham never lived to see the fulfilment of the promise precisely because the fulfilment, in the view of Hebrews, is on a spiritual level and took place centuries later in Jesus.

(Vv. 17–18)

In Jewish tradition, Abraham underwent ten testings, the tenth and greatest of which was the command to sacrifice Isaac. In his willingness to sacrifice Isaac in Genesis 22, Abraham never abandoned the promise but staked his life on 'things hoped for, things unseen.' Notice the built-in ambiguity: he offered and he was ready to offer. Thus he is a model of faithful endurance for the readers who are also being tested now.

(V. 19)

The author alludes to the shocking test of Abraham in Genesis 22. For the author, the sacrifice of Isaac, like the other stories in the list, is an indication that people continue to live by faith in God's promises, despite the reality of death. Isaac was as good as dead until God gave him back to his father: Jewish tradition uses various approaches to make moral sense of this 'text of terror'. In Hebrews, Abraham is taken to be motivated by faith in the resurrection of dead. Although clearly anachronistic, resurrection faith was originally trust in the faithfulness of God himself. In later Jewish tradition, a connection was drawn between resurrection and the '*Akedah*' (the 'binding of Isaac' Genesis 22), and some Jewish sources even suggest that Abraham actually sacrificed Isaac, who was then resurrected by God. In Christian allegory, Isaac came to be seen as a type foreshadowing Christ, in both sacrifice and return from the dead.

Pointers for prayer

a) The fuller reading lists the great heroes of the faith. We can all name those who have guided us and inspired us. Who would be on your list? Are you yourself a source of inspiration and guidance?

b) Faith, in the Abraham stories, means trusting against the evidence and against the odds. While this is not everything one would wish to say about faith, still from time to time sheer endurance can be a significant part of our faith journey. Am I able to name contexts and times when this was true for me?

c) The starry vision offered to Abraham seems simply too good to be true … and yet, sometimes we feel the faith is *so* good that it just *has* to be true. Such times of conviction and even exuberance are mostly likely rare … but significant all the same. Is there some special moment I look back to for reassurance and hope?

d) Our reading takes 'the long view', that is, over the whole of salvation history. What about the long view of my own journey of faith and salvation?

Prayer

God of Sarah and Abraham, you call us all to go beyond what we can see or even imagine. Strengthen our trust, give life to our faith and make our steadfastness joyful and life-giving. Help us, companion God, to know your presence with us throughout the pilgrimage of faith. Give us the assurance of things hoped for and the conviction of things not seen. Thus, like Abraham, may we place all our trust in you, through Jesus, the pioneer of our faith, who lives and reigns for ever and ever. Amen.

🌿 First Reading (1) 🌿

Gen 15:1 After these things the word of the L ORD came to Abram in a vision, 'Do not be afraid, Abram, I am your shield; your reward shall be very great.' [2] But Abram said, 'O Lord G OD, what will you give me, for I continue childless, and the heir of my house is Eliezer of Damascus?' [3] And Abram said, 'You have given me no offspring, and so a slave born in my house is to be my heir.' [4] But the word of the L ORD came to him, 'This man shall not be your heir; no one but your very own issue shall be your heir.' [5] He brought him outside and said, 'Look toward heaven and count the stars, if you are able to count them.' Then he said to him, 'So shall your descendants be.' [6] And he believed the L ORD; and the L ORD reckoned it to him as righteousness.

Gen 21:1 The L ORD dealt with Sarah as he had said, and the L ORD did for Sarah as he had promised. [2] Sarah conceived and bore Abraham a son in his old age, at the time of which God had spoken to him. [3] Abraham gave the name Isaac to his son whom Sarah bore him.

Initial observations

The reading is about childlessness and the desire to have children. It is, therefore, a delicate subject on the feast of the Holy Family. Some in our faith community will know what is it like to want children and not to be able have them. Any introduction to the reading will have to bear this is in mind.

Within the narrative, the impatience of Abram is perfectly understandable: he has heard this promise before and now, according to the narrative, he is somewhere between seventy-five and one hundred! In Genesis 12:4 Abram is seventy-five when he sets out; in Genesis 16:16 he is eighty-six when Ishmael is born; in Genesis 17:1 he is ninety-nine when birth of Isaac is promised which happens the following year; finally, in Genesis 21:5, Abraham is one hundred when

Isaac was born. He has another seventy-five years (Genesis 25:7) to go, so it's not so bad after all.

Kind of writing

(i) The first part of Genesis 15 shows the following sequence

The word of the Lord	v. 1	Promise of reward
The word of Abram	vv. 2–3	Complaint about no children
The Lord's' response	v. 4	Promise of an heir
A public act	v. 5a	Taken into the open air
The word of the Lord	v. 5b	Promise of many descendants
Abram's response	v. 6	Abram's faith

(ii) The first part of Genesis 21 shows the following sequence
>   Birth of Isaac (1–2),
>   Naming (3),
>   Circumcision (4),
>   Abraham's age (5),
>   Sarah's comments (6–7).

The basic story is told without much detail or even emotion. Emotion (and how!) is reserved for the next tale of the jealousy between the mothers and their sons (Genesis 21:8–21). Sarah manages to turn around the play of words on laughter from Genesis 18:12–15.

Origin of the reading

The reading offers portions of Genesis 15 and 21, leaving the impression that not much has happened in between. However, it is well recognised that the three great cycles of stories in Genesis (Abraham, Jacob and Joseph) have been written, edited and structured with care and a not inconsiderable artistry. The Abraham cycle, for instance, shows a large concentric outline. The core scenes are laid out thus:

Sodom episode and rescue of Lot (14:1–24)
>   Covenant of sacrifice (15:1–21)
>>   Expulsion and rescue of Hagar (16:1–16)
>   Covenant of circumcision (17:1–27)

Sodom episode and rescue of Lot (18:1–19:38)

Genesis 15 is to be read in the light of Genesis 12 and 17.

Related passages

I will bless her, and moreover I will give you a son by her. I will bless her, and she shall give rise to nations; kings of peoples shall come from her.' Then Abraham fell on his face and laughed, and said to himself, 'Can a child be born to a man who is a hundred years old? Can Sarah, who is ninety years old, bear a child?' And Abraham said to God, 'O that Ishmael might live in your sight!' God said, 'No, but your wife Sarah shall bear you a son, and you shall name him Isaac. I will establish my covenant with him as an everlasting covenant for his offspring after him. As for Ishmael, I have heard you; I will bless him and make him fruitful and exceedingly numerous; he shall be the father of twelve princes, and I will make him a great nation. But my covenant I will establish with Isaac, whom Sarah shall bear to you at this season next year.' (Genesis 17:16–21)

Then one said, 'I will surely return to you in due season, and your wife Sarah shall have a son.' And Sarah was listening at the tent entrance behind him. Now Abraham and Sarah were old, advanced in age; it had ceased to be with Sarah after the manner of women. So Sarah laughed to herself, saying, 'After I have grown old, and my husband is old, shall I have pleasure?' The Lord said to Abraham, 'Why did Sarah laugh, and say, 'Shall I indeed bear a child, now that I am old?' Is anything too wonderful for the Lord? At the set time I will return to you, in due season, and Sarah shall have a son.' But Sarah denied, saying, 'I did not laugh'; for she was afraid. He said, 'Oh yes, you did laugh.' (Genesis 18:10–15)

Brief commentary

(V. 1)

'After these things' makes a link with the preceding chapter. The word of the coming to someone is a prophetic idiom as in 1 Samuel 15:10; Hosea 1:1. Abraham is himself called a prophet in Genesis 20:7. Shield is often used of God: Psalm 84:12–13; Proverbs 30:5.

(V. 2)

Lord GOD = Adonai YHWH, a rare form (only here and in 15:8 in Genesis). Abram's complaint is very clear, after all the promises. The Hebrew, rendered here as 'and the heir of my house is Eliezer of Damascus', is very unclear both in terms of the word and the person.

(V. 3)

This verse seems to duplicate v. 2 and may be an early attempt to deal with the obscurity there.

(V. 4)

This is an emphatic denial – very direct in Hebrew. 'Look' suggests a long look; cf. 1 Kings 18:43; Exodus 3:6.

(V. 5)

Abram's descendants are always said to be numberless, using different metaphors (Genesis 12:2; 13:15; 15:5; 16:10; 17:2, 4; 22:17).

(V. 6)

This is really a comment on the preceding verse, without which it would be hard to know how Abram reacted. The form in Hebrew may well indicate repeated or continuing action, thus a response typical of Abram. Righteousness can be helpfully rendered as 'right relationship' or acting rightly within the expected parameters of a relationship. Faith, in the sense of trust, is the right response to God's action and promise. This verse was fully exploited by Paul, of course.

(V. 1)

Literally, the Lord 'visited' Sarah. The 'visits' of God always indicate a special interest of God in that person. The promises referred to are Genesis 17:16–21 and 18:10–15.

(V. 2)

Even if you live to be 175, ninety-nine is still old! The precision of the fulfilment is noted.

(V. 3)

Abraham follows God's instructions exactly: 'God said, "No, but your wife Sarah shall bear you a son, and you shall name him Isaac. I will establish my covenant with him as an everlasting covenant for his off-spring after him".' (Genesis 17:19) The name Isaac comes from the root 'to laugh'.

Pointers for prayer

a) Like many people in the Bible, Abram is told not to be afraid – a constant reassurance which implies fear, of course. When do I feel the need for such consolation in my own life?

b) The story tells of a promise repeatedly given and long post-poned. Have there been good and natural things in my own life that I have had to wait long for?

c) Abraham – our 'father in faith' – placed all his trust in God and this, of itself, was sufficient. When have I found that trust, pure faith, makes all the difference?

d) Sarah and Abraham finally have a child – and Sarah's joy is evident in her healing laughter. Recall your own joy when a son or daughter was born.

Prayer

Giver of every good gift, faithful God, we thank you for your faithfulness and love, which excel all we ever knew of you. As we await the fulfilment of all your promises in Jesus, help us to place all our trust in you. Through Christ our Lord. Amen.

🌿 First Reading (2) 🌿

Sir 3:3 Those who honour their father atone for sins, ⁴ and those who respect their mother are like those who lay up treasure. ⁵ Those who honour their father will have joy in their own children, and when they pray they will be heard. ⁶ Those who respect their father will have long life, and those who honour their mother obey the Lord; ⁷ they will serve their parents as their masters.

Sir 3:14 For kindness to a father will not be forgotten, and will be credited to you against your sins; ¹⁵ in the day of your distress it will be remembered in your favour; like frost in fair weather, your sins will melt away. ¹⁶ Whoever forsakes a father is like a blasphemer, and whoever angers a mother is cursed by the Lord. ¹⁷ My child, perform your tasks with humility; then you will be loved by those whom God accepts.

Initial observations

This is a very fitting reading for the feast. In the lectionary, the shortened version is quite coherent and makes sense. However, the omitted verses, while somewhat negative, may reflect reality!

Kind of writing

Sirach is wisdom instruction, in the form of poetry with plenty of parallelism. In our reading, there isn't much by way of metaphor but there are lots of synonyms for honour and for the marks of old age. V. 15 – not in the lectionary – contains a striking image of frost melting. The full poem runs to sixteen verses, sensibly abbreviated, given the quantity of repetition. There seem to be three stanzas: vv. 1–7, 8–11 and 12–16.

Origin of the reading

Sirach was written originally in Hebrew and then translated into Greek for the benefit of Jews living in Egypt. The book itself tells us about its production and formation. There is a prologue by Ben Sira's grandson, which introduces the whole book. He goes on to say: *When I came to Egypt in the thirty-eighth year of the reign of Euergetes and stayed for some time, I found opportunity for no little instruction. It seemed highly necessary that I should myself devote some diligence and labour to the translation of this book. During that time I have applied my skill day and night to complete and publish the book for those living abroad who wished to gain learning and are disposed to live according to the law.*

At the end of the book, there is an autobiographical poem, in which we read:

Instruction in understanding and knowledge I have written in this book, Jesus son of Eleazar son of Sirach of Jerusalem, whose mind poured forth wisdom (Sirach 50:27.)

The book itself – a late example of biblical Wisdom – may seem conservative. For example, regarding the problem of evil, it knows nothing of the radical perspective of Job and, frankly, it can be misogynist. On the other hand, it does contain a quite remarkable theology of creation and Wisdom. Some of the very best biblical resources for a theology of creation can be found in this book. See for instance Sirach 42:22–43:33. The author's astonishment before creation and the creator is well captured in these words: 'We could say more but could never say enough; let the final word be: "He is the all"' (Sirach 43:27). This is risky writing and could sound pantheist but he gets away with it because elsewhere the transcendence of God is clearly affirmed.

Related Passages

Honour your father and your mother, so that your days may be long in the land that the Lord your God is giving you. (Exodus 20:12)

Honour your father and your mother, as the Lord your God commanded you, so that your days may be long and that it may go well with you in the land that the Lord your God is giving you. (Deuteronomy 5:16)

Whoever curses father or mother shall be put to death. (Exodus 21:17)

Then Tobit called his son Tobias, and when he came to him he said, 'My son, when I die, give me a proper burial. Honour your mother and do not abandon her all the days of her life.

Do whatever pleases her, and do not grieve her in anything. Remember her, my son, because she faced many dangers for you while you were in her womb. And when she dies, bury her beside me in the same grave.' (Tobit 4:3–4)

Hear, my child, your father's instruction, and do not reject your mother's teaching; for they are a fair garland for your head, and pendants for your neck. (Proverbs 1:8–9)

Brief commentary

(Vv. 3–4)
The parallelism is apparent. Cf. *Lay up your treasure according to the commandments of the Most High, and it will profit you more than gold. Store up almsgiving in your treasury, and it will rescue you from every disaster* (Sirach 29:11–12).

(V. 5)
The first part reflects experience: children learn from their parents how to respect parents.

(V. 6)
This echoes the reward attached to honouring parents: Honour your father and your mother, so that your days may be long in the land that the Lord your God is giving you. (Exodus 20:12; cf. Deuteronomy 5:16.) There is a related commandment with a not dissimilar reward (an irony not lost on the rabbis): *If you come on a bird's nest, in any tree or on the ground, with fledglings or eggs, with the mother sitting on the fledglings or on the eggs, you shall not take the mother with the young. Let the mother go, taking only the young for yourself, in order that it may go well with you and you may live long* (Deuteronomy 22:6–7).

(V. 14)
The same sentiment is found in v. 3 above.

(V. 15)
V. 15b repeats v. 15a, but with a delightful recollection of the warmth of spring causing frost to melt away.

(V. 16)

This blunt verse echoes an even more blunt text in Exodus: 'Whoever curses father or mother shall be put to death' (Exodus 21:17).

Pointers for prayer

a) Is it true that if people 'honour' a parent, they have joy in their own children? What do you think the link is? What has your own experience been?

b) The verse about the mind failing is, alas, true in the experience of many. It is a challenge to continue to be loving and sensitive, to honour and show respect. What has your experience been and what did you learn about yourself?

Prayer

Great and loving God, you are to us a father and a mother. Help us to continue to love and respect our parents, for in honouring them we honour you, from whom all parenthood takes its name. We make this prayer through our Lord Jesus Christ, who lives and reigns for ever and ever. Amen.

Themes across the readings

Families are endlessly fascinating: so much of who we are comes from family and stays with us all our lives. Of course there is darkness, limitation, conflict, all sorts of inherited things. But there is also light, possibility, love and healing grace. It all depends on how we choose to go on from here.

Chapter 10

Second Sunday of Christmas B

Thought for the day

We are at the start of the new civil year and beginning again is an invitation to look in two directions. What happened for me in the last year, both in my ordinary life and in my life as a believer, a person of faith? For what do I ask forgiveness? For what do I give thanks? We also look forward and the new beginning gives us a chance to start again on the Way of discipleship. Both thanksgiving and renewal are to be found in today's readings. The gospel is in invitation to wake up, to keep watch, to live fully the present moment under God, in whom we live and move and have our being.

Prayer

Wake us up, O God, at the start of a new year and rouse us from the slumber of the everyday that we may recognise you in every moment and in every person every day of our lives. Through Christ our Lord. Amen.

🌿 Gospel 🌿

Jn 1:1 In the beginning was the Word, and the Word was with God, and the Word was God. [2] He was in the beginning with God. [3] All things came to be through him, and without him nothing came to be. What came to be [4] through him was life, and this life was the light of the human race; [5] the light shines in the darkness, and the darkness has not overcome it. [6] A man named John was sent from God. [7] He came for testimony, to testify to the light, so that all might believe through him. [8] He was not the light, but came to testify to the light. [9] The true light, which enlightens everyone, was coming into the world.

[10] He was in the world, and the world came to be through him, but the world did not know him. [11] He came to what was his own, but his own people did not accept him. [12] But to those who did accept him he gave power to become children of God, to those who believe in his name, [13] who were born not by natural generation nor by human choice nor by a man's decision but of God.

[14] And the Word became flesh and made his dwelling among us, and we saw his glory, the glory as of the Father's only Son, full of grace and truth.

[15] John testified to him and cried out, saying, 'This was he of whom I said, "The one who is coming after me ranks ahead of me because he existed before me."' [16] From his fullness we have all received, grace in place of grace, [17] because while the law was given through Moses, grace and truth came through Jesus Christ. [18] No one has ever seen God. The only Son, God, who is at the Father's side, has revealed him.

The only Son, God, who is at the Father's side, has revealed him.

Initial observations

The Prologue was already commented on for the third Mass of Christmas Day (see notes there). For today, a different translation (New American Bible Revised Edition) and a different commentary will be offered.

Kind of writing

Our reading is poetry – Wisdom poetry – with insistent prose interruptions.

Old Testament background

It would be a great help to look up these passages about 'Lady Wisdom': Job 28; Proverbs 1, 8, 9; Baruch 3:9–4:4; Sirach 24; Wisdom 7:7–9:18.

New Testament foreground

We declare to you what was from the beginning, what we have heard, what we have seen with our eyes, what we have looked at and touched with our hands, concerning the word of life – this life was revealed, and we have seen it and testify to it, and declare to you the eternal life that was with the Father and was revealed to us – we declare to you what we have seen and heard so that you also may have fellowship with us; and truly our fellowship is with the Father and with his Son Jesus Christ. We are writing these things so that our joy may be complete. (1 John 1:1–4)

Beloved, do not believe every spirit, but test the spirits to see whether they are from God; for many false prophets have gone out into the world. By this you know the Spirit of God: every spirit that confesses that Jesus Christ has come in the flesh is from God, and every spirit that does not confess Jesus is not from God. And this is the spirit of the antichrist, of which you have heard that it is coming; and now it is already in the world. Little children, you are from God, and have conquered them; for the one who is in you is greater than the one who is in the world. (1 John 4:1–4)

St Paul

But when the appropriate time had come, God sent out his Son, born of a woman, born under the law, to redeem those who were under the law, so that we may be adopted as sons with full rights. And because you are sons, God sent the Spirit of his Son into our hearts, who calls '*Abba*! Father!' So you are no longer a slave but a son, and if you are a son, then you are also an heir through God. (Galatians 4:4–7)

Brief commentary

The commentary takes the form of showing where the topics and images occur again throughout the gospel. Thus, the function of the Prologue as a true introduction becomes clear.

(V. 1)

New Creation: When Jesus had received the wine, he said, 'It is finished.' Then he bowed his head and gave up his spirit (John 19:30). When he had said this, he breathed on them and said to them, 'Receive the Holy Spirit' (John 20:22). Cf. John 20:1.

(V. 2)

Union with the Father: The Father and I are one (John 10:30). So now, Father, glorify me in your own presence with the glory that I had in your presence before the world existed (John 17:5).

(V. 3)

Through him: No one comes to the Father except through me (John 14:6). Indeed, God did not send the Son into the world to condemn the world, but in order that the world might be saved through him (John 3:17).

(V. 4)

Life and light: I am the way, and the truth, and the life (John 14:6). Jesus said to her, 'I am the resurrection and the life. Those who believe in me, even though they die, will live, and everyone who lives and believes in me will never die (John 11:25–26). And this is eternal life, that they may know you, the only true God, and Jesus Christ whom you have sent (John 17:3).

(V. 5)

Light and darkness: And this is the judgement, that the light has come into the world, and people loved darkness rather than light because their deeds were evil (John 3:19). Again Jesus spoke to them, saying, 'I am the light of the world. Whoever follows me will never walk in darkness but will have the light of life' (John 8:12).

(V. 6–8)
John the Baptist: Cf. John 1:19–23.

(V. 9)
Into the world: 'When the people saw the sign that he had done, they began to say, "This is indeed the prophet who is to come into the world"' (John 6:14). 'She said to him, "Yes, Lord, I believe that you are the Messiah, the Son of God, the one coming into the world"' (John 11:27). 'Pilate asked him, "So you are a king?" Jesus answered, "You say that I am a king. For this I was born, and for this I came into the world, to testify to the truth. Everyone who belongs to the truth listens to my voice"' (John 18:37).

(V. 10)
Did not receive him: 'This is the Spirit of truth, whom the world cannot receive, because it neither sees him nor knows him. You know him, because he abides with you, and he will be in you' (John 14:17).

(V. 11)
Opposition of his own: 'The man went away and told the Jews that it was Jesus who had made him well. Therefore the Jews started persecuting Jesus, because he was doing such things on the sabbath' (John 5:15–17). 'The Jews then disputed among themselves, saying, "How can this man give us his flesh to eat?"' (John 6:52) 'The Jews said to him, "Now we know that you have a demon. Abraham died, and so did the prophets; yet you say, 'Whoever keeps my word will never taste death'"' (John 8:52). 'The Jews answered, "It is not for a good work that we are going to stone you, but for blasphemy, because you, though only a human being, are making yourself God"' (John 10:33). 'The Jews answered him, "We have a law, and according to that law he ought to die because he has claimed to be the Son of God"' (John 19:7).

(V. 12)
Children of God: 'He did not say this on his own, but being high priest that year he prophesied that Jesus was about to die for the nation, and not for the nation only, but to gather into one the dispersed children of God' (John 11:51–52). 'While you have the light, believe in the light, so that you may become children of light' (John 12:36). Cf. John 21:5.

(V. 13)

Born of God: 'Jesus answered him, "Very truly, I tell you, no one can see the kingdom of God without being born from above." Nicodemus said to him, "How can anyone be born after having grown old? Can one enter a second time into the mother's womb and be born?" Jesus answered, "Very truly, I tell you, no one can enter the kingdom of God without being born of water and Spirit. What is born of the flesh is flesh, and what is born of the Spirit is spirit. Do not be astonished that I said to you, 'You must be born from above.' The wind blows where it chooses, and you hear the sound of it, but you do not know where it comes from or where it goes. So it is with everyone who is born of the Spirit'" (John 3:3–8). Cf. John 15:4–5.

(V. 14)

Glory, grace, truth: 'Father, I desire that those also, whom you have given me, may be with me where I am, to see my glory, which you have given me because you loved me before the foundation of the world' (John 17:24). 'From his fullness we have all received, grace upon grace. The law indeed was given through Moses; grace and truth came through Jesus Christ' (John 1:16–17). 'But the hour is coming, and is now here, when the true worshippers will worship the Father in spirit and truth, for the Father seeks such as these to worship him. God is spirit, and those who worship him must worship in spirit and truth' (John 4:23–24). 'When the Spirit of truth comes, he will guide you into all the truth; for he will not speak on his own, but will speak whatever he hears, and he will declare to you the things that are to come' (John 16:13). 'Pilate asked him, "So you are a king?" Jesus answered, "You say that I am a king. For this I was born, and for this I came into the world, to testify to the truth. Everyone who belongs to the truth listens to my voice." Pilate asked him, "What is truth?"' (John 18:37–38).

Dwell: note the Jewish festival of Booths (= skēnopēgia, matching eskēnōsen 'dwelt' in 1:14) was near (John 7:2).

(V. 15)

He existed before me: 'This is he of whom I said, "After me comes a man who ranks ahead of me because he was before me"' (John 1:30). 'Now a discussion about purification arose between John's disciples and a Jew. They came to John and said to him, "Rabbi, the one who was with you across the Jordan, to whom you testified, here he is baptising, and all are going to him." John answered, "No one can receive anything except what has been given from heaven. You yourselves are my witnesses that I said, 'I am not the Messiah, but I have been sent ahead of him.' He who has the bride is the bridegroom. The friend of the bridegroom, who stands and hears him, rejoices greatly at the bridegroom's voice. For this reason my joy has been fulfilled. He must increase, but I must decrease'" (John 3:25–30). 'Jesus said to them, "Very truly, I tell you, before Abraham was, I am'" (John 8:58).

(V. 16)
Fullness: 'I came that they may have life, and have it abundantly' (John 10:10). 'I have said these things to you so that my joy may be in you, and that your joy may be complete' (John 15:11). 'But now I am coming to you, and I speak these things in the world so that they may have my joy made complete in themselves' (John 17:13).

(V. 17)
Moses: 'Do not think that I will accuse you before the Father; your accuser is Moses, on whom you have set your hope. If you believed Moses, you would believe me, for he wrote about me' (John 5:45–46). 'Then Jesus said to them, "Very truly, I tell you, it was not Moses who gave you the bread from heaven, but it is my Father who gives you the true bread from heaven'" (John 6:32). 'Moses gave you circumcision (it is, of course, not from Moses, but from the patriarchs), and you circumcise a man on the sabbath. If a man receives circumcision on the sabbath in order that the law of Moses may not be broken, are you angry with me because I healed a man's whole body on the sabbath?' (John 7:22–23). 'Then they reviled him, saying, "You are his disciple, but we are disciples of Moses. We know that God has spoken to Moses, but as for this man, we do not know where he comes from'" (John 9:28–29).

(V. 18)
Make known: 'Not that anyone has seen the Father except the one who is from God; he has seen the Father' (John 6:46). 'I do not call you

servants any longer, because the servant does not know what the master is doing; but I have called you friends, because I have made known to you everything that I have heard from my Father' (John 15:15). 'I have made your name known to those whom you gave me from the world. They were yours, and you gave them to me, and they have kept your word' (John 15:15; 17:6). 'I made your name known to them, and I will make it known, so that the love with which you have loved me may be in them, and I in them' (John 17:26).

Pointers for prayer

a) John opens his gospel with a profound reflection on the meaning of creation, of life and of Jesus. Remember when you had a special awareness of the gift of life that filled you with gratitude to God for creation and the beauty and wonder of the world: 'All things came into being through him and without him not one thing came into being.'

b) We hear the Gospel message frequently. Sometimes it goes in one ear and out the other. Then there are occasions when it made us feel more alive, times when it helped us see the way ahead, like a light that shines in the darkness. Recall when the Gospel gave you hope in the midst of anxiety or sadness and helped you to see what action would be most life giving for you and for others

c) Bring to mind people who have had a prophetic voice in the world – speaking the truth for the world to hear, like a witness testifying to the light. Some of these may have been public figures. Others were ordinary people who have helped you see the 'light' by the witness of their own lives and words.

d) 'No one has ever seen God. It is the only Son of God, who is close to the Father's heart, who has made him known.' Jesus came to us to teach us about God and put a human face on God for us. For the people of his day, and for us, that was a mission of getting us to think again about how we see God and to believe in a God who is a God of love. Recall how the life and ministry of Jesus have changed your picture of God.

Prayer

God most high, your only Son embraced the weakness of our flesh to give us the power to become your children; your eternal Word chose to dwell among us, that we might live in your presence.

Grant us a spirit of wisdom to know how rich is the glory you have made our own, and how great the hope to which we are called in Jesus Christ, the Word made flesh who lives and reigns with you in the unity of the Holy Spirit in the splendour of eternal light, God for ever and ever. Amen.

🌿 Second Reading 🌿

Eph 1:3 Blessed be the God and Father of our Lord Jesus Christ, who has blessed us in Christ with every spiritual blessing in the heavenly places, [4] just as he chose us in Christ before the foundation of the world to be holy and blameless before him in love. [5] He destined us for adoption as his children through Jesus Christ, according to the good pleasure of his will, [6] to the praise of his glorious grace that he freely bestowed on us in the Beloved.

Eph 1:15 I have heard of your faith in the Lord Jesus and your love towards all the saints, and for this reason [16] I do not cease to give thanks for you as I remember you in my prayers. [17] I pray that the God of our Lord Jesus Christ, the Father of glory, may give you a spirit of wisdom and revelation as you come to know him, [18] so that, with the eyes of your heart enlightened, you may know what is the hope to which he has called you, what are the riches of his glorious inheritance among the saints, [19] *and what is the immeasurable greatness of his power for us who believe, according to the working of his great power.*

Initial observations

This reading offers us another opportunity within the Christmas season to reflect once more on what the birth of Jesus could mean for us today.

While both parts of the reading do this, there is a special fervour in the second prayer. The air is invitatory: come and see what the Lord has done ...

Kind of writing

In the genuine letters from Paul, the epistolary format has been adjusted to include a longer thanksgiving for the faith of the recipients. In 2 Corinthians this takes the form of a 'blessing' prayer. In Ephesians, both styles are present.

vv. 3–14 Blessing prayer
vv. 15–23 Thanksgiving report

Our reading takes in excerpts from both. The entire passage should be read; it seems a pity that the lectionary needlessly omits v. 19. Sensibly, the Revised Common Lectionary offers vv. 3–14 as the reading. In contrast to the genuine letters, there is no implied account of what is happening in the community.

Origin of the reading

It is not quite sure if this letter should be addressed to the Ephesians, because some important manuscripts lack the expression 'in Ephesus'. It has also proved difficult to establish the context in the community that occasioned the writing. (i) Is it to do with the famous and flourishing Artemis cult? (ii) It is to do with proto-gnostic mythologies? (iii) Or perhaps, some combination involving Jewish speculation on the heavenly journey? A clue is provided by the Dead Sea Scrolls, suggesting a Jew with a background in Jewish sectarianism. At the same time, the writing is very polished, so a Jew who enjoyed a good Hellenistic education (not unlike the apostle himself). Perhaps in a context of flourishing Judaism, the writer tries to bolster Christian identity. In any case, the vision is breath-taking, taking us well beyond the limits of the Roman Empire to a global expansion of the Gospel.

Related passages

> In our prayers for you we always thank God, the Father of
> our Lord Jesus Christ, for we have heard of your faith in

Christ Jesus and of the love that you have for all the saints. (Colossians 1:3–4)

When I remember you in my prayers, I always thank my God because I hear of your love for all the saints and your faith toward the Lord Jesus. (Philemon 1:4–5)

Brief commentary

(V. 3)

Praise is the foundational attitude of prayer in the Bible, often taking the form 'blessed be God'. The expression 'every spiritual blessing' is especially rich: in contrast to human givers, God's gift is everything we need. It also places the Ephesians on the same level as the angels. The prayer will go on to describe Jesus in cosmic language; nevertheless, it begins with Jesus the Messiah.

(V. 4)

Christian vocation itself is to be found in the pre–existence of Christ, in whom we were already chosen. The divine will is underlined in vv. 4–5, 9 and 11. The idea that all humanity is in view is also found in the Dead Sea Scrolls. 'In love' will be echoed in the 'beloved' of v. 6.

(Vv. 5–6)

Here the writer takes up the Pauline theme of adoption (Romans 8:15–23; Galatians 4:4–7). In contrast with Qumran, there is no reference at all to the predestination of the wicked. Predestination texts are also found in Paul: Romans 8:29–30 and 1 Corinthians 2:7. The pronouns are indicative: *he* and *his*. All is centred on God, a highly theocentric presentation of salvation. V. 6 tells us why all this took place: *to the praise of his glorious grace.*

(Vv. 15–16)

The reputation of the recipients is not boasting or flattery but a means of evangelisation, leading naturally to thanksgiving. Cf. 1 Thessalonians 1:3–12 and 2 Corinthians 8:1–2.

(V. 17)

The writer moves from a thanksgiving report to intercession. God's wisdom was already mentioned: *In him we have redemption through his blood, the forgiveness of our trespasses, according to the riches of his grace that he lavished on us. With all wisdom and insight he has made known to us the mystery of his will, according to his good pleasure that he set forth in Christ, as a plan for the fullness of time, to gather up all things in him, things in heaven and things on earth* (Ephesians 1:7–10). The Spirit of wisdom probably ought to have a capital letter, pointing to a more than human wisdom.

(V. 18)

The language here is very close to that of the Essenes: *May He enlighten your mind with wisdom for living, be gracious to you with the knowledge of eternal things, and lift up His gracious countenance upon you for everlasting peace.* (1Qs [= The Community Rule] 2:3–4) The eyes of your heart is unparalleled elsewhere but seems to suggest moral conduct. The content of that enlightenment is expanded in terms of Christian hope. Saints means simply fellow Christians, as opposed to angels.

Pointers for prayer

a) How would my own prayer of blessing unfold? For what would I give thanks from the bottom of my heart?

b) The reputation of any community of faith is important – for the sake of the Gospel. Where does my community stand?

Prayer

God of wisdom and light, send your Holy Spirit into our hearts that we may be your children in name and in fact and thereby draw others into the great adventure of faith, hope and love in you. Through Christ our Lord. Amen.

🍃 First Reading 🍃

Sir 24:1   Wisdom praises herself,
      and tells of her glory in the midst of her people.

2   In the assembly of the Most High she opens her mouth,
      and in the presence of his hosts she tells of her glory:

8   'Then the Creator of all things gave me a command,

> and my Creator chose the place for my tent.
> He said, "Make your dwelling in Jacob,
> > and in Israel receive your inheritance."
>
> 9   Before the ages, in the beginning, he created me,
> > and for all the ages I shall not cease to be.
>
> 10   In the holy tent I ministered before him,
> > and so I was established in Zion.
>
> 11   Thus in the beloved city he gave me a resting place,
> > and in Jerusalem was my domain.
>
> 12   I took root in an honoured people,
> > in the portion of the Lord, his heritage.'

Initial observations

Sirach 24 is one of the great texts for the personification of Lady Wisdom.

Kind of writing

The poem is laid out in three stanzas, with an introduction and a series of conclusions.

vv. 1–2 *Introduction*
vv. 3–7 (I) Pre–existent wisdom
vv. 8–12 (II) *Wisdom dwells in Jerusalem*
vv.13–17 (III) Horticultural metaphors
vv. 18–22 Viticulture and its fruits
vv. 23–29 Prose reflection
vv. 30–34 The poet's authority

Vv. 23–34 help us grasp the writer's goal.

Prose reflection

All this is the book of the covenant of the Most High God, the law that Moses commanded us as an inheritance for the congregations of Jacob. It overflows, like the Pishon, with wisdom, and like the Tigris at the time of the first fruits. It runs over, like the Euphrates, with understanding, and like the Jordan at harvest time. It pours forth instruction like the

Nile, like the Gihon at the time of vintage. The first man did not know wisdom fully, nor will the last one fathom her. For her thoughts are more abundant than the sea, and her counsel deeper than the great abyss. (Sirach 24:23–29)

The poet's authority

As for me, I was like a canal from a river, like a water channel into a garden. I said, 'I will water my garden and drench my flower–beds.' And lo, my canal became a river, and my river a sea. I will again make instruction shine forth like the dawn, and I will make it clear from far away. I will again pour out teaching like prophecy, and leave it to all future generations. Observe that I have not laboured for myself alone, but for all who seek wisdom. (Sirach 24:30–34)

Origin of the reading

Sirach is a late Wisdom book, emphasising 'God in everything.' It was written in Hebrew – only partially extant – but it survives in its integrity in Greek.

Related passages

The passage seems to draw upon Proverbs 8, as well as Job 28. For another reflection on Wisdom, see Proverbs 1:20–33.

Wisdom cries out in the street; in the squares she raises her voice. At the busiest corner she cries out; at the entrance of the city gates she speaks: 'How long, O simple ones, will you love being simple? How long will scoffers delight in their scoffing and fools hate knowledge? Give heed to my reproof; I will pour out my thoughts to you; I will make my words known to you. Because I have called and you refused, have stretched out my hand and no one heeded, and because you have ignored all my counsel and would have none of my reproof, I also will laugh at your calamity; I will mock when panic strikes you, when panic strikes you like a storm, and your calamity comes like a whirlwind, when distress and anguish come upon you. Then they will call upon me, but I will not answer; they will seek me diligently, but will not find me. Because they hated knowledge and did not choose the fear of the LORD, would have none of my counsel, and despised all my reproof, therefore they shall eat the fruit of their way and be sated with their own devices. For waywardness kills the simple, and the complacency of fools destroys them; but those who listen to me will be secure and will live at ease, without dread of disaster.' (Proverbs 1:20–33)

Brief commentary

Every religion has to 'negotiate' the beyond and the nearness of God, his transcendence and his immanence, in technical vocabulary. Judaism achieved this by speaking of Wisdom, from the beyond in God, but present in all that exists.

(V. 1)
Praising yourself might seem strange but such poems are found widely ('aretologies'). 'Her people' will eventually be Israel and not just humanity.

(V. 2)
Initially, we are in the heavenly court, where Wisdom exists already.

(V. 8)
The reading was chosen in part because of the word tent (*skēnē*), also found in John 1:14 above. The language of dwelling etc. is picked up in the Prologue very well. Cf. Proverbs 8:22. For a contrasting understanding: *Wisdom could not find a place in which she could dwell; but a place was found (for her) in the heavens. Then Wisdom went out to dwell with the children of the people, but she found no dwelling place. (So) Wisdom returned to her place and she settled permanently among the angels* (1 Enoch 42:1–2).

(V. 9)
In other writings, Wisdom seems to pre-exist before creation and even be the very mind of God. In any case, there is something of the divine about her.

(V. 10)

God's presence is recognised in the Temple in Jerusalem (a special interest of Sirach).

V. 11

Concretely, Wisdom – the *shekinah* in the *skēnē* – is found in the Holy City, in the Holy of Holies.

(V. 12)

Thus Wisdom is present not only in the Temple but also in the Torah. Cf. *All this is the book of the covenant of the Most High God, the law that Moses commanded us as an inheritance for the congregations of Jacob* (Sirach 24:23).

Pointers for prayer

a) God in all that is: Recall your own awareness of how near the Lord is to us all – and give thanks.

b) Recall your own deep moments when the presence of God was somehow 'apparent' to you in his living word.

Prayer

God, closer to us than we are to ourselves and yet always greater than our hearts, help us to remain in your presence: through your Wisdom in all that is and through Jesus, our wisdom, righteousness, sanctification and redemption. Through the same Christ our Lord. Amen.

Themes across the readings

We continue to reflect on what happened for us in the birth of Jesus in Bethlehem. All the readings invite us to 'think big'. At the time Ephesians was composed, the number of Christians around Ephesus was really small but their hope, their vision was large. The closing prayer says it all: *May the God of our Lord Jesus Christ, the Father of glory, give you a spirit of wisdom and perception of what is revealed, to bring you to full knowledge of him. May he enlighten the eyes of your mind so that you can see what hope his call holds for you, what rich glories he has promised the saints will inherit* (Ephesians 1:17–18 NJB).

Chapter 11

The Epiphany of the Lord B

Thought for the day

In our deepest selves, each of us is a mystery: Where do I come from? Where am I going? Why am I here? How should I live? The risk in our present culture is to sleepwalk through life, to be satisfied with a merely sentient, even material, existence. But the human 'project' is much greater. Each of us is really on a pilgrimage or, better, on a quest – a quest to become my true self, in the image and likeness of God. My truest self is found by being open to God, in whom we live and move and have our being. By following that star, by listening to our conscience and inner selves, we come home to God.

Prayer

You are the mystery at the heart of all that exists: draw us to yourself, O Lord, that knowing you we find our true selves, and finding our true selves, we may come to know you. Through Christ our Lord. Amen.

🌿 Gospel 🌿

Mt 2:1 In the time of King Herod, after Jesus was born in Bethlehem of Judea, wise men from the East came to Jerusalem, ² asking, 'Where is the child who has been born king of the Jews? For we observed his star at its rising, and have come to pay him homage.' ³ When King Herod heard this, he was frightened, and all Jerusalem with him; ⁴ and calling together all the chief priests and scribes of the people, he inquired of them where the Messiah was to be born.

⁵ They told him, 'In Bethlehem of Judea; for so it has been written by the prophet:

⁶ "And you, Bethlehem, in the land of Judah, are by no means least among the rulers of Judah; for from you shall come a ruler who is to shepherd my people Israel."'

⁷ Then Herod secretly called for the wise men and learned from them the exact time when the star had appeared. ⁸ Then he sent them to Bethlehem, saying, 'Go and search diligently for the child; and when you have found him, bring me word so that I may also go and pay him homage.' ⁹ When they had heard the king, they set out; and there, ahead of them, went the star that they had seen at its rising, until it stopped over the place where the child was. ¹⁰ When they saw that the star had stopped, they were overwhelmed with joy. ¹¹ On entering the house, they saw the child with Mary his mother; and they knelt down and paid him homage. Then, opening their treasure chests, they offered him gifts of gold, frankincense and myrrh. ¹² And having been warned in a dream not to return to Herod, they left for their own country by another road.

Initial observations

The readings from the Infancy Gospels bear an unusually close link to narratives in the Old Testament. Again, the writer is exploring the identity of Jesus, using citations and rewritten narratives. It all may seem strange to us, but the original hearers – Jewish Christians – would have had no trouble picking up the resonances and going straight to the meaning expressed in the stories.

Kind of writing

As usual with the infancy narratives, this is a kind of *haggadah*, a rabbinic style of writing which explores and exposes meaning by a resonant acoustic of echoes, thereby creating devotional and uplifting literature. Everything is in some way symbolic – the star, the magi, the king, Bethlehem and the gifts – pointing to the identity of Jesus and the inclusion of the Gentiles in salvation.

Old Testament background

(i) Behind the story of the magi – wise men – lies the story of Balaam from Numbers 22–24. In the book of Numbers, an evil king of Moab tries to use the seer/magus Balaam to bring disaster on the people of Israel 'because they were so numerous. Against God's will, Balaam obeys the king, but at the point of cursing Israel, Balaam utters an oracle of future hope. This oracle was read in later times as a Messianic promise.

> I see him, but not now; I behold him, but not near – a star shall come out of Jacob, and a sceptre shall rise out of Israel (Numbers 24:17).

The author takes from this story the narrative of an evil king (Balak/Herod), trying to bring disaster (on Israel/on the Messiah), by means of Balaam (a seer/the Magi). The star in the story comes from Numbers 24:17 above and alerts the reader, this time to Messianic fulfilment.

(ii) The gifts offered by the magi call to mind a universalist text in Isaiah:

> A multitude of camels shall cover you, the young camels of Midian and Ephah; all those from Sheba shall come. They shall bring gold and frankincense, and shall proclaim the praise of the Lord (Isaiah 60:6).

It was concluded from this text as well that the mode of transport of the magi was camels, although Matthew supplies no such detail.

(iii) The Magi as a symbol of the Gentiles comes from an echo in Psalm 72:

> May the kings of Tarshish and of the isles render him tribute, may the kings of Sheba and Seba bring gifts. May all kings fall down before him, all nations give him service (Psalm 72:10–11).

(iv) Bethlehem, the city of David, is mentioned frequently in the Old

Testament, unlike Nazareth. The proof text provided was, at the time, read as a messianic prophecy.

> But you, O Bethlehem of Ephrathah, who are one of the little clans of Judah, from you shall come forth for me one who is to rule in Israel, whose origin is from of old, from ancient days (Micah 5:2).

New Testament foreground

(i) Matthew's Gospel reflects the historical memory that Jesus did not himself directly evangelise the Gentiles, at least initially.

> These twelve Jesus sent out with the following instructions: 'Go nowhere among the Gentiles, and enter no town of the Samaritans, but go rather to the lost sheep of the house of Israel' (Matthew 10:5–7).

(ii) Nevertheless, in Matthew's Gospel and community, the Gentiles are an important audience of the Good News: Matthew (15); Mark (6); Luke (13); John (5).

[a] At the start of the ministry: 'Now when Jesus heard that John had been arrested, he withdrew to Galilee. He left Nazareth and made his home in Capernaum by the sea, in the territory of Zebulun and Naphtali, so that what had been spoken through the prophet Isaiah might be fulfilled: "Land of Zebulun, land of Naphtali, on the road by the sea, across the Jordan, Galilee of the Gentiles – the people who sat in darkness have seen a great light, and for those who sat in the region and shadow of death light has dawned." From that time Jesus began to proclaim, "Repent, for the kingdom of heaven has come near"' (Matthew 4:12–17).

[b] During the ministry: 'When Jesus became aware of this, he departed. Many crowds followed him, and he cured all of them, and he ordered them not to make him known. This was to fulfil what had been spoken through the prophet Isaiah: "Here is my servant, whom I have chosen, my beloved, with whom my soul is well pleased. I will put my Spirit upon him, and he will proclaim justice to the Gentiles. He will

not wrangle or cry aloud, nor will anyone hear his voice in the streets. He will not break a bruised reed or quench a smouldering wick until he brings justice to victory. And in his name the Gentiles will hope'" (Matthew 12:15–21).

[c] At the close of the Gospel: Now the eleven disciples went to Galilee, to the mountain to which Jesus had directed them. When they saw him, they worshiped him; but some doubted. And Jesus came and said to them, 'All authority in heaven and on earth has been given to me. Go therefore and make disciples of all nations, baptising them in the name of the Father and of the Son and of the Holy Spirit, and teaching them to obey everything that I have commanded you. And remember, I am with you always, to the end of the age' (Matthew 28:16–20).

St Paul

> Now to God who is able to strengthen you according to my gospel and the proclamation of Jesus Christ, according to the revelation of the mystery that was kept secret for long ages but is now disclosed, and through the prophetic writings is made known to all the Gentiles, according to the command of the eternal God, to bring about the obedience of faith – to the only wise God, through Jesus Christ, to whom be the glory for ever! Amen. (Romans 16:25–27)

Brief commentary

Once the Old Testament correspondences and the Gospel anticipations have been uncovered the text practically comments itself. Nevertheless (!):

(V. 1)
This is King Herod the Great, who died in 4 BC. The 'wise men' are literally 'magi'. Magus, a Persian loan word, covers a range of meanings: wise man and priest, who was expert in astrology, interpretation of dreams and various other occult arts. From the East: traditionally, the source of wisdom.

(V. 2)

The Gentiles identify universal hope in the Jewish Messiah and king.

(V. 3)

The historical Herod was quite paranoid about usurpers and even had some of his sons killed. Augustus said of him: 'I would prefer to be his pig (*hus*) than his son (*huios*).'This was after Herod put his two favourite sons, Aristobolus and Alexander, to death (he had already executed their mother, his favourite wife Mariamne). He was an exceptionally unstable, not to say murderous, spouse and parent.

(V. 5)

Matthew has Bible experts (like himself) identify the birthplace of the Messiah, with a proof – text from Micah. 'Shepherd' reminds us of David, the great symbol of God's faithfulness through time.

(V. 7)

The (f)rank hypocrisy of Herod links this symbolic tale with the massacre of the innocents to follow.

(V. 10)

Joy comes back in Matthew 28:8 at the empty tomb. For other uses, see Matthew 2:10; 13:20, 44; 25:21, 23.

(V. 11)

Fulfilling Psalm 72 and Isaiah 60, as noted above.

(V. 12)

With no further narrative use for them, the Magi are taken 'off stage' somewhat peremptorily.

Pointers for prayer

a) What is the star (the vision, hope or purpose) that lights up your journey?

b) Like the wise men, our life journey is not one we travel alone. Who are the people who share your life journey now?

c) The wise men travelled bearing gifts. What gift do you bring with you on the journey?

d) At times the wise men lost sight of the star. What clouds have obscured your star?

e) Who, or what, might be Herod for you now? What forces, within or without, could subvert the dream or goal?

Prayer

Lord God of the nations, we have seen the star of your glory rising in splendour. The radiance of your incarnate Word pierces the darkness that covers the earth and signals the dawn of peace and justice. Make radiant the lives of your people with that same brightness, and beckon all the nations to walk as one in your light. We ask this through Jesus Christ, your Word made flesh, who lives and reigns with you in the unity of the Holy Spirit, in the splendour of eternal light, God for ever and ever. Amen.

🌿 Second Reading 🌿

Eph 3:1 *This is the reason that I Paul am a prisoner for Christ Jesus for the sake of you Gentiles –* ² for surely you have already heard of the commission of God's grace that was given me for you, ³ and how the mystery was made known to me by revelation, as I wrote above in a few words, ⁴ *a reading of which will enable you to perceive my understanding of the mystery of Christ.* ⁵ In former generations this mystery was not made known to humankind, as it has now been revealed to his holy apostles and prophets by the Spirit: ⁶ that is, the Gentiles have become fellow heirs, members of the same body, and sharers in the promise in Christ Jesus through the gospel.

Initial observations

In liturgical tradition, the epiphany embraces no fewer than three gospel stories: the Magi, the Baptism and the Wedding Feast at Cana. Each of these is a kind disclosure or revelation. The feast, then, celebrates something 'being made known' or revealed and the reading from Ephesians is thus especially fitting.

Kind of writing

It can be tricky to follow the sequence of prayer and digression in Ephesians. In the view of many, Ephesians 3:2–13 forms a digression on the origin of Paul's gospel and apostleship. That is apparent from the abruptness of v. 2. V. 1 itself is an attempt to pick up a much earlier intercession from 1:16–19. But 3:1 is itself then subject to a digression, and the prayer will be completed only in 3:14–19. It may help to see a recomposed sequence as follows:

Eph 1:16 I do not cease to give thanks for you as I remember you in my prayers. [17] I pray that the God of our Lord Jesus Christ, the Father of glory, may give you a spirit of wisdom and revelation as you come to know him, [18] so that, with the eyes of your heart enlightened, you may know what is the hope to which he has called you, what are the riches of his glorious inheritance among the saints, [19] and what is the immeasurable greatness of his power for us who believe, according to the working of his great power. **Eph 3:1** This is the reason that I Paul am a prisoner for Christ Jesus for the sake of you Gentiles – **Eph 3:14** For this reason I bow my knees before the Father, [15] from whom every family in heaven and on earth takes its name. [16] I pray that, according to the riches of his glory, he may grant that you may be strengthened in your inner being with power through his Spirit, [17] and that Christ may dwell in your hearts through faith, as you are being rooted and grounded in love. [18] I pray that you may have the power to comprehend, with all the saints, what is the breadth and length and height and depth, [19] and to know the love of Christ that surpasses knowledge, so that you may be filled with all the fullness of God.

Origin of the reading

As noted elsewhere, there is a discussion about the Pauline authorship of this letter. A common solution is that the text was written by a disciple of Paul, after the apostle's death, to bring his teaching to bear in a new and later context. The reasons for doubting Pauline authorship include the vocabulary, the theology and the unusual relationship with Colossians.

Related passage

> But now in Christ Jesus you who once were far off have been brought near by the blood of Christ. For he is our peace; in his flesh he has made both groups into one and has broken down the dividing wall, that is, the hostility between us. He has abolished the law with its commandments and ordinances, that he might create in himself one new humanity in place of the two, thus making peace, and might reconcile both groups to God in one body through the cross, thus putting to death that hostility through it. So he came and proclaimed peace to you who were far off and peace to those who were near; for through him both of us have access in one Spirit to the Father. (Ephesians 2:13–18)

Brief commentary

(V. 1)

The writer begins a prayer but it continues with the same words from v. 14 onwards.

(V. 2)

The word commission can also be found here: 'as a *plan* for the fullness of time, to gather up all things in him, things in heaven and things on earth' (Ephesians 1:10), 'and to make everyone see what is the plan of the mystery hidden for ages in God who created all things' (Ephesians 3:9). Thus, Paul's ministry is part of a wider commission or plan. This commission was given *to* Paul *for* others. It is presumed the hearers are familiar with Paul.

(V. 3)

Mystery is used in a different sense across the Pauline corpus and is evidently more common in the Deutero-Pauline letters: Romans 11:25; 16:25; 1 Corinthians 2:1, 7; 4:1; 13:2; 14:2; 15:51; *Ephesians 1:9; 3:3–4, 9; 5:32; 6:19; Colossians 1:26–27; 2:2; 4:3; 2 Thessalonians 2:7; 1 Timothy 3:9, 16*. It refers to the unity of Jews and Gentiles in the one people of God, already firmly established by the time of writing. See the important Ephesians 2:13–18 above. For revelation see Galatians 1:11–12, 15–16. Daniel 2 is also part of the background.

(V. 4)

Omitted in the lectionary for the sake of clarity, this verse sends the hearers back to the whole Pauline mission and theology. This grasp of God's plan, entrusted to an individual, is then discerned and appropriated by the Church as whole.

(V. 5)

This amounts to a denial of a pattern found widely in the New Testament and in Paul, that is, that the Scripture *foretells* and Christians then *confirm*. For our author, the revelation is new and made through the spiritual agents of the Christian community. Cf. *I became its servant according to God's commission that was given to me for you, to make the word of God fully known, the mystery that has been hidden throughout the ages and generations but has now been revealed to his saint.* (Colossians 1:25–26).

(V. 6)

This verse compresses what has been said more fully in Ephesians 2:13–18. Note the vocabulary of heirs, body, promise and gospel, all genuine Pauline expressions. Cf. Ephesians 2:19. 'In' means 'by means of', an instrumental use.

Pointers for prayer

a) Disclosure and wonder are both present, inviting reflection on my own moments of revelation and awe.

b) On my own journey of faith, who have been the 'apostles', the ones sent who have helped me see the hope to which we are called?

Prayer

O the depth of the riches and wisdom and knowledge of God! How unsearchable are his judgements and how inscrutable his ways!

'For who has known the mind of the Lord? Or who has been his counsellor?'

'Or who has given a gift to him, to receive a gift in return?'

For from him and through him and to him are all things. To him be the glory for ever. Amen.

(Romans 11:33–36)

🌿 First Reading 🌿

Is 60:1   'Arise! Shine! For your light arrives!
        The splendour of the LẑRD shines on you!
2   For, look, darkness covers the earth
        and deep darkness covers the nations,
        but the LẑRD shines on you;
        his splendour appears over you.
3   Nations come to your light,
        kings to your bright light.
4   Look all around you!
        They all gather and come to you –
        your sons come from far away
        and your daughters are escorted by guardians.
5   Then you will look and smile,
        you will be excited and your heart will swell with pride.
        For the riches of distant lands will belong to you
        and the wealth of nations will come to you.
6   Camel caravans will cover your roads,
        young camels from Midian and Ephah.
        All the merchants of Sheba will come,
        bringing gold and incense
        and singing praises to the LẑRD.'

Initial observations

As even a cursory glance will reveal, the reading is extremely well chosen. Firstly, because of the symbolism of light (more below). Secondly, because of the gathering/coming together of all the faithful. Following a very early intuition based on this text and Psalm 72, the reading adds pictorially both the *royal* status of the Magi and their mode of *transport*. The mention of gold and frankincense probably inspired the imaginative filling in of these details. Notice also that *three* places are mentioned.

Kind of writing

The writing is poetry and in this case it is almost a textbook example of 'parallelism', whereby the second line repeats the first, but in more concrete, sometimes more elaborate vocabulary. For example, vv. 1 and 2 or v. 5.

Our excerpt comes from a longer section (Isaiah 60:1–62:12) and even within that the subsection 60:1–22 offers a poem on the light of the Lord. This is in response to Isaiah 59:9–10, which reads: *Therefore justice is far from us, and righteousness does not reach us; we wait for light, and lo! there is darkness; and for brightness, but we walk in gloom. We grope like the blind along a wall, groping like those who have no eyes; we stumble at noon as in the twilight, among the vigorous as though we were dead* (Isaiah 59:9–10).

Origin of the reading

Isaiah 60 comes from Third Isaiah, a prophet or prophets writing in the tradition of Isaiah of Jerusalem, but reflecting a much later situation after the return from the exile in Babylon.

Related passages

> Then your light shall break forth like the dawn, and your healing shall spring up quickly; your vindicator shall go before you, the glory of the LORD shall be your rear guard. (Isaiah 58:8)

> ... if you offer your food to the hungry and satisfy the needs of the afflicted, then your light shall rise in the darkness and your gloom be like the noonday. (Isaiah 58:10)

> Therefore justice is far from us, and righteousness does not reach us; we wait for light, and lo! there is darkness; and for brightness, but we walk in gloom. (Isaiah 59:9)

> The sun shall no longer be your light by day, nor for brightness shall the moon give light to you by night; but the LORD will

be your everlasting light, and your God will be your glory. Your sun shall no more go down, or your moon withdraw itself; for the LORD will be your everlasting light, and your days of mourning shall be ended. (Isaiah 60:19–20)

Brief commentary

To illustrate the theological integrity of this composite book, it may be sufficient to observe that there are many echoes, in the whole of Isaiah 60:1–22, of earlier passages in Isaiah.

(V. 1)
This text presumes that the Temple has been rebuilt and that all peoples will come there to worship. Here it is no longer God who will be their light: they themselves are light and they should shine. Cf. Matthew 5:14–15.

(V. 2)
After v. 2a, the repetition in v. 2b refers to the shadow of death or deadly darkness. The Lord's glory is not so much his splendour as the full presence of God.

(V. 3)
Notice the delightful evolution of the poetry: not just nations but also kings; not just light but also the brightness of your dawn.

(V. 4)
Cf. Isaiah 40:10–11. At this point, the addressees seem to be at home in Jerusalem, perhaps in the Temple. Very young children are envisaged.

(V. 5)
V. 5ab expresses the spontaneous joy, even exhilaration, at the prospect of salvation. V. 5cd might seem rather greedy, but it is an echo from the book of Exodus, reflecting the despoilment of the Egyptians before departure (Exodus 12:13–36). In any case, the bringing of gifts fits the feast. Midian is associated with the Gulf of Aqaba, as is Ephah. Sheba is in the south-west of (modern) Arabia. In any case, a substantial distance is imagined.

(V. 6)

Cf. Isaiah 40:5. This is where we get the idea that camels are part of the story! The gold and frankincense of v. 6c are intended for worship, as v. 6d makes clear. Frankincense is a resin, mentioned in both the Old Testament and New Testament as a highly desired and esteemed product. The trade collapsed in the fifth century, after the Muslims forbade its use at funerals.

Pointers for prayer

a) Although the passage is indeed about light, it does acknowledge the need of light as we experience darkness. Not only do we need light, we are to *be* light, as Matthew 5 puts it.

b) The reading is exuberant, to a degree we might find hard to rise to, and yet, joy is truly part of our faith experience.

c) It all culminates in praise of the Lord, that spontaneous gratitude towards God who has loved us so much as to be one of us, the great mystery of Christmas.

d) The sense of pilgrimage, homecoming, is very much part of the reading and, of course, part of Christian imagination. Think only of *Pilgrim's Progress*. Reflect on your one journey of faith, until today.

Prayer

We praise you, God, for the gift of light in creation, sunlight and moonlight, illuminating all you have made. Above all we thank you for the light of Christ, that you have shone in our hearts. May we welcome this light and became bearers of your light to all around us. Through Christ our Lord. Amen.

Themes across the readings

In the tradition, the magi were later given names, personalities and biographies. The temptation to continue to 'fill in' proved irresistible. We may smile, but the instinct is good because the magi stand for real people – you and me – people on a spiritual quest, hearers of the word, listening out for a potential word from the Mystery, now disclosed.

Chapter 12

The Baptism of the Lord B

Thought for the day

In all our lives, there are 'before and after' moments, whatever they might be (parenthood, marriage, career etc.). In my life as a disciple, can I name any particular 'before and after' moments? This probably won't include baptism, because most of us were just babies, but later, what happened to bring faith alive and help me grow up as a believer? Such reflection may help us grasp the significance of John's baptism for Jesus himself. For him, it was a true 'before and after' event, sustained by the ringing affirmation, 'You are my Son, the Beloved; with you I am well pleased.'

Prayer

Father, we are all your beloved sons and daughters; we dare to say that with us too you are well pleased. Help us embrace our new reality by letting ourselves be loved by you. Through Christ our Lord. Amen.

Gospel

Mk 1:7 [John] proclaimed, 'The one who is more powerful than I is coming after me; I am not worthy to stoop down and untie the thong of his sandals. ⁸ I have baptised you with water; but he will baptise you with the Holy Spirit.'

⁹ In those days Jesus came from Nazareth of Galilee and was baptised by John in the Jordan. ¹⁰ And just as he was coming up out of the water, he saw the heavens torn apart and the

Spirit descending like a dove on him. [11] And a voice came from heaven, 'You are my Son, the Beloved; with you I am well pleased.'

Initial observations

That John the Baptist baptised Jesus is historically certain. As the New Testament unfolds, there is increasing unease with this fact, revealed in the editorial strategies of Matthew, Luke and John. Such unease arose, in part, from the continued existence of followers of John the Baptist right up to the end of the first century. When we link this fact with the other fact, namely, that the timing of Jesus' own ministry is triggered by the arrest of John the Baptist, then it is safe to conclude that Jesus was a follower of John the Baptist and did not go into the desert just to be immersed by him. The metaphorical relatedness of the two figures is intriguingly explored by Luke in his first two chapters.

It is important to establish who John the Baptist was. In summary, a prophetic figure, in the mould of the iconic prophet Elijah; he withdrew from the Temple cult into the desert because of the compromised nature of the priesthood; he preached the coming Kingdom of God, an experience of judgement; historically, he may or may not have recognised Jesus. (The stories in John 1 are driven by theology, not by history.) As a follower, Jesus echoed his mentor's teaching.

In those days John the Baptist appeared in the wilderness of Judea, proclaiming, 'Repent, for the kingdom of heaven has come near' (Matthew 3:1–2).

From that time Jesus began to proclaim, 'Repent, for the kingdom of heaven has come near' (Matthew 4:17).

The similarity is evident. However, whereas John preached *judgement and conversion*, Jesus preached *the good news and conversion*. Finally, Mark 1:8, as it stands, reflects Christian theology. It is likely that John originally used a comparison of water and fire, as follows: 'I have baptised you with water; but he will baptise you with fire' (Mark 1:8).

Kind of writing

The excerpt in the lectionary takes in two scenes. The first is the presentation of John the Baptist (1:2–8) and the second is the prophetic legitimation of Jesus (1:9–12). In continuity with the biblical tradition, this legitimation is presented as a theophany, with visual and acoustic symbols. Note that only Jesus sees and hears the symbolic phenomena – as well as, significantly, the reader. The reader attends to the rest of the story differently on account of this privileged knowledge about the identity of Jesus.

Old Testament background

> Then he sent out the dove from him, to see if the waters had subsided from the face of the ground; but the dove found no place to set its foot, and it returned to him to the ark, for the waters were still on the face of the whole earth. So he put out his hand and took it and brought it into the ark with him. He waited another seven days, and again he sent out the dove from the ark; and the dove came back to him in the evening, and there in its beak was a freshly plucked olive leaf; so Noah knew that the waters had subsided from the earth. Then he waited another seven days, and sent out the dove; and it did not return to him any more. (Genesis 8:8–12)

> Lo, I will send you the prophet Elijah before the great and terrible day of the Lord comes. (Malachi 4:5)

> I will tell of the decree of the Lord: He said to me, 'You are my son; today I have begotten you. (Psalm 2:7)

> Here is my servant, whom I uphold, my chosen, in whom my soul delights; I have put my spirit upon him; he will bring forth justice to the nations. (Isaiah 42:1)

> He said, 'Take your son, your only son Isaac, whom you love, and go to the land of Moriah, and offer him there as a burnt

offering on one of the mountains that I shall show you.' (Genesis 22:2)

New Testament foreground

(a) John the Baptist turns up a few more times in Mark: the arrest and death of John (6:14–29); the comparison with Jesus (6:14–15; 8:28); the authority of John (11:27–33). There is a fuller picture in Matthew and Luke.

(b) Related events in Jesus' life: the words at the Transfiguration and after the death of Jesus.

> Then a cloud overshadowed them, and from the cloud there came a voice, 'This is my Son, the Beloved; listen to him!' (Mark 9:6–8)

> Now when the centurion, who stood facing him, saw that in this way he breathed his last, he said, 'Truly this man was God's Son!' (Mark 15:39)

St Paul

> Do you not know that all of us who have been baptised into Christ Jesus were baptised into his death? Therefore we have been buried with him by baptism into death, so that, just as Christ was raised from the dead by the glory of the Father, so we too might walk in newness of life. (Romans 6:3–4)

> For all of you who were baptised into Christ have clothed yourselves with Christ. There is neither Jew nor Greek, there is neither slave nor free, there is neither male nor female – for all of you are one in Christ Jesus. And if you belong to Christ, then you are Abraham's descendants, heirs according to the promise. (Galatians 3:27–29)

Brief commentary

(V. 7)

'Proclaimed' (whence *kerygma*) is a very important word in the New Testament, especially in Paul. Mark uses it proportionately much more frequently: Matthew (9); Mark (14); Luke (9); John (0); Acts (8). In Christian terms, it implies effective proclamation, especially in the ministry of Jesus himself and in the proclamation of Paul. Historically, John the Baptist did look forward to another figure, but there is some uncertainty as to whom (the messiah? God? a prophet? an angel? etc.). That John was unworthy to undertake the most menial task of a slave speaks for itself. Footwear remains the image in Matthew, although there John is not worthy *to carry* his sandals. Even Mark feels the need to emphasise the inferiority of John to Jesus.

(V. 8)

Immersion is found in almost all religions and, of course, in Judaism. The distinctive feature of John's immersion was that it was a one-off and that it expressed a commitment to his vision and the consequent conversion of heart and life. (Needless to mention, this immersion is to be distinguished from the later Christian baptism.) The original word pair was probably water and fire (see Matthew 3:11–12), a more natural contrast and a fitting one for the rather ferocious Baptist. Later Christian experience of Spirit, symbolised by fire, has facilitated the editorial adjustment.

(V. 9)

The bare facts are coolly reported here. This was clearly a highly significant choice for Jesus and the next few verses interpret the event. Mark has no discussion like that in Matthew, because in this gospel Jesus identifies with sinners – cf. Isaiah 6:5; 53:12. Isaiah continues to be the influence in the next verses: God's spirit rest upon the prophet (Isaiah 61:1), he is the servant/son (Isaiah 42:1) and the ideal Davidic ruler (Isaiah 11:1–3).

(V. 10)

The heavens torn apart: that is, an ecstatic, transcendent experience. It had been generally conceded by then that from the point of view of prophecy and revelation, the heavens were shut. The most one could hope for was an echo of God's voice (the *bat qol*, literally, the daughter of a voice). The sense of vocation and anointing, undoubtedly historical, is expressed symbolically through the Spirit descending. Was it the Spirit *like a dove* descending? Or was it, the Spirit *descending like* a dove? The iconographic tradition privileges the literal, but the metaphorical may be more accurate. Just as the dove signalled the end of the disaster of the flood, here the Spirit, descending on Jesus as he rises from the 'flood', signals the end of that silence of the closed heavens. The driving force of this Spirit is immediately evident in v. 12. The (Holy) Spirit is mentioned a few times in Mark. Just now on the lips of John the Baptist (v. 8); the driver into the desert (1:12); the sin against the Holy Spirit (3:9); the inspiration of Scripture (12:36); the giver of the right words in times of persecution (13:11).

(V. 11)

A voice from heaven resembles Daniel 4:31, an apocalyptic book. The first words are a citation from Psalm 2:7 (perhaps also Isaiah 42:1 above), an important source for early Christological reflection (Acts 13:33; Hebrews 1:5; 5:5). Beloved has a double reference. It indicates someone unique and at the same time someone especially loved and cherished. There is a disturbing echo of Genesis 22:2, where Abraham is commanded to sacrifice his beloved son. 'Delights' is limited to here in Mark. The link with the transfiguration is intentional: *Then a cloud overshadowed them, and from the cloud there came a voice, 'This is my Son, the Beloved; listen to him!'* (Mark 9:7)

Pointers for prayer

a) John gives an example of humility as a person confident in his own role but not seeking to claim to be more than he is. He is able to acknowledge that Jesus is greater. There is a freedom in being able to acknowledge the gifts of others without losing a sense of one's own giftedness. Recall times when you were able to do this.

b) The baptism of Jesus was an extraordinary religious experience for him. Something happened that was a major step forward for Jesus in coming to know that he was *the* beloved Son of God. We all have events in our lives that are milestones along the road of discovering who we are. What have been these milestones for you?

c) 'You are my Son, the Beloved; with you I am well pleased.' Bring to mind memories of experiences in which you knew you were the beloved (of God or of another person) and that the one who loved you was well pleased. Bring these experiences to mind with gratitude, knowing that the only proper response to love received is thankfulness. Perhaps you have also given that experience to another.

Prayer

God of salvation, in the River Jordan you bathed your Son Jesus in glory and revealed him as your obedient servant. In spirit and in power rend the heavens and come down to us. Strengthen us to acknowledge your Christ, that we who are reborn in his likeness may walk with him in newness of life. Grant this through Jesus Christ, your Word made flesh, who lives and reigns with you in the unity of the Holy Spirit, in the splendour of eternal light, God for ever and ever. Amen.

🌿 Second Reading 🌿

1 Jn 5:1 Everyone who believes that Jesus is the Christ has been born of God, and everyone who loves the parent loves the child. [2] By this we know that we love the children of God, when we love God and obey his commandments. [3] For the love of God is this, that we obey his commandments. And his commandments are not burdensome, [4] for whatever is born of God conquers the world. And this is the victory that conquers the world, our faith. [5] Who is it that conquers the world but the one who believes that Jesus is the Son of God?

[6] This is the one who came by water and blood, Jesus Christ,

not with the water only but with the water and the blood. And the Spirit is the one that testifies, for the Spirit is the truth. [7] There are three that testify: [8] the Spirit and the water and the blood, and these three agree. [9] If we receive human testimony, the testimony of God is greater; for this is the testimony of God that he has testified to his Son.

Initial observations

The insistence upon faith, water, the Spirit and testimony makes this a suitable reading for the feast of the baptism of the Lord. The general insistence across the letter on the true humanity of Jesus makes it also suitable to mark the close of the Christmas season.

Kind of writing

1 John is not exactly a letter and not exactly a homily, but it does exhibit features of both. Many would consider it an 'epistolary sermon.'

1:1–4	PROLOGUE
1:5–2:17	*Exhortation*
2:18–27	Affirmations
2:28–3:24	*Exhortations*
4:1–6	Affirmations
4:7–5:5	*Exhortations*
5:6–12	Affirmations
5:13–21	EPILOGUE

In this scheme, the lectionary reading straddles two sections, moving from exhortations to affirmations.

Origin of the reading

Much about this document is disputed: authorship, location, genre and so forth. What is not really disputed is the context. It reflects an early deformation of Christianity which diminished both the humanity and divinity of Jesus. There had been conflict in the community and some had departed/been expelled. It may also be that some regarded themselves to be so spiritual that ethical behaviour somehow no longer mattered. This would account for the repeated tone of exhortation.

Related passages

> Beloved, I am writing you no new commandment, but an old commandment that you have had from the beginning; the old commandment is the word that you have heard. Yet I am writing you a new commandment that is true in him and in you, because the darkness is passing away and the true light is already shining. (1 John 2:7–8)

> All who obey his commandments abide in him, and he abides in them. And by this we know that he abides in us, by the Spirit that he has given us. (1 John 3:24; cf. 4:6, 13.)

> When the Advocate comes, whom I will send to you from the Father, the Spirit of truth who comes from the Father, he will testify on my behalf. (John 15:26)

> In your law it is written that the testimony of two witnesses is valid. I testify on my own behalf, and the Father who sent me testifies on my behalf. (John 8:17–18)

Brief commentary

(V 1)

This is very like John 1:12–13; 3:3–5 etc. It is an incomplete syllogism, with the 'therefore' part implied, perhaps even triggered within!

(Vv. 2–3a)

The author rehearses teaching familiar from the Johannine tradition, with its great emphasis on love of God and of each other. It includes, nevertheless, thoroughly ethical behaviour following the commandments.

(Vv. 3b–4)

Why are the commandments not burdensome? The author reflected on this in 1 John 2:7–8 above. The believer has a different energy, that of victorious faith, through the Spirit.

(V. 5)

The faith that is truly victorious believes Jesus to be the Son of God. The high doctrine of the Johannine 'school' certainly triggered schisms. Cf. *Simon Peter answered him, 'Lord, to whom can we go? You have the words of eternal life. We have come to believe and know that you are the Holy One of God'* (John 6:68–69). The extreme interpretation of that led to early Docetism, the error that Jesus only seemed (*dokeō*) to be human. The orthodox response is expressed in the simple verb: *he came*, but in the aorist tense, i.e. he came once for all in the incarnation.

(V. 6)

Before going straight for a sacramental interpretation of this verse, it is good to remember that in the Fourth Gospel the order is blood and water, i.e. the death of Jesus and the new life flowing from it. Thus it serves to affirm the true humanity of Jesus. At a second remove, the passage then hints – in correct order – at baptism and eucharist. Added to the witness of Jesus' real death, there is the witness of the Spirit (see the citations above).

(Vv. 7–8)

The witness is powerful because threefold and from God himself.

(Vv. 9)

Witness/testimony is characteristic Johannine vocabulary: Matthew (1); Mark (0); Luke (1); John (33); 1 John (6). The verse is an a fortiori argument. Not to accept God's testimony is to treat God as a liar. See John 8:17–18 above.

Pointers for prayer

a) The connecting up of faith, love and obedience is very strong and invites reflection on my integration of obedience, love and faith in my own discipleship.

b) Both John and Paul teach that total Christian living is possible – once we surrender ourselves fully to the Spirit of the Son. It does put it up to us …

c) All spiritual testimony comes mediated and must be tested.

And yet, it must also be a reality for each of us on the journey, so not only 'tested' but tested and tried in life.

Prayer

God, our loving parent, help us to love you in each other and so love you and live the greatest commandment.

Send your Holy Spirit that we may know from within the victory of faith and so live lives of courageous witness to Jesus, our brother, the Son of God, who lives and reigns with you and the Spirit, one God, for ever and ever. Amen.

❧ First reading ❧

Is 55:1 Ho, everyone who thirsts, come to the waters; and you that have no money, come, buy and eat! Come, buy wine and milk without money and without price. ² Why do you spend your money for that which is not bread, and your labour for that which does not satisfy? Listen carefully to me, and eat what is good, and delight yourselves in rich food. ³ Incline your ear, and come to me; listen, so that you may live. I will make with you an everlasting covenant, my steadfast, sure love for David. ⁴ See, I made him a witness to the peoples, a leader and commander for the peoples. ⁵ See, you shall call nations that you do not know, and nations that do not know you shall run to you, because of the LORD your God, the Holy One of Israel, for he has glorified you. ⁶ Seek the LORD while he may be found, call upon him while he is near; ⁷ let the wicked forsake their ways, and the unrighteous their thoughts; let them return to the LORD, that he may have mercy on them, and to our God, for he will abundantly pardon. ⁸ For my thoughts are not your thoughts, nor are your ways my ways, says the LORD. ⁹ For as the heavens are higher than the earth, so are my ways higher than your ways and my thoughts than your thoughts. ¹⁰ For as the rain and the snow come down from heaven, and do not return there until they have watered the earth, making it bring forth and sprout, giving seed to the sower and bread to the eater, [11] so shall my word be that goes out from my mouth; it shall not return to me empty, but it shall accomplish that which I purpose, and succeed in the thing for which I sent it.

Initial observations

The first reading is an extended, very rich invitation to come back to God. A link between the readings is established by the use of the word 'return' in Isaiah 55:7. Return means conversion and repentance, that is, *metanoia*.

Kind of writing

This prophetic oracle shows the usual feature of poetic parallelism. Isaiah 55:1–9 are almost completely in parallel verses with the exception of 5bc. The pleasure of this writing is in the variant expression of the same thought, either with higher literary terms or by more concrete language. Isaiah 55:10–11 vary the pattern a little and constitute a kind of extended parable, using the imagery of rainfall and 'automatic' growth. It is one of the most well-remembered passages from the book of Isaiah.

Origin of the reading

Isaiah 40–55, part of the composite book of Isaiah, was written towards the end of the Babylonian Exile (cf. Isaiah 55:12–13).

Related passage

See the detailed commentary below for the Old Testament roots of the imagery. The final verses of Isaiah 55 continue in the same spirit, where even nature itself undergoes a transformation:
Isaiah 55:12   For you shall go out in joy,
> and be led back in peace;
the mountains and the hills before you
> shall burst into song,
> and all the trees of the field shall clap their hands.

13   Instead of the thorn shall come up the cypress;
                 instead of the briar shall come up the myrtle;
        and it shall be to the LORD for a memorial,
                 for an everlasting sign that shall not be cut off.

Brief commentary

(V. 1)

The 'ho' ('hey' in the NET, which sounds very contemporary!) at the start is usually negative, but here it seems to be positive. Thirsting is a common image for the spiritual journey (for example, Psalm 42:1–2; 63:1; 143:6). Buying without money is an oxymoron, underscoring the gift and grace of God.

(V. 2)

V. 2d is literally 'Enjoy the fatness'. We might translate, 'enjoy your meal'. The rich food stands for all the gifts of God given through the covenant. The contrast is with what is not *really* food, food that does not really *satisfy*.

(V. 3)

As often, the ear stands for the receptivity of the whole person. Life is the fruit of faithfulness to the covenant (see Deuteronomy 30:6, 15, 19–20). The permanence of the covenant is often noticed (Genesis 9:16; 17:7; 2 Samuel 23:5 etc.). The sure love for David is underlined in 2 Samuel 7 and Psalm 89. In Second Isaiah, the role of David is figuratively given to the people (as there was no Davidic monarch at the time). The reference underlines faithful continuity amidst tremendous change – probably as challenging then as now!

(V. 4)

This takes up the servant role somewhat. See Isaiah 45:14, 22–24; 49:6.

(V. 5)

Holy One of Israel is found earlier: *The sinful nation is as good as dead, the people weighed down by evil deeds. They are offspring who do wrong, children who do wicked things. They have abandoned the Lord, and rejected the Holy One of Israel. They are alienated from him* (Isaiah 1:4). Israel is to become God's beacon to other nations –unlikely in the contemporary political setting. See the savage irony of Romans 2:17–24.

(Vv. 6–7)
Vv. 6 and 7 constitute a great call to repentance, echoing Deuteronomy 4:25–31; 30:1–10; and 1 Kings 8:46–53. These passages anticipate the Exile and speak of the conditions for restoration.

(Vv. 8–9)
Vv. 8 and 9, justly famous, echo similar themes across the Bible. Cf. *For as the heavens are high above the earth, so great is his steadfast love toward those who fear him* (Psalm 103:11; also Romans 11:33–36).

(V. 10)
The dependence on the seasonal rains makes this metaphor especially powerful and evocative.

(V. 11)
The association of the word with the forces of nature recalls the creation by word in Genesis 1. God's *word* is effective because it is *God's* word. Cf. Isaiah 45:23; 46:10; 53:10.

Pointers for prayer

a) The note of gracious, freely given gift is present throughout. Explore your own 'human' experience of such free gifts, especially through people who come into your life. Unearned love comes closest and even opens our heart to the gift of God.

b) The contrasting idea is not to waste your time and energy on what does not lead to life. What experiences of life have helped you to realise this yourself? As Augustine put it, our hearts are restless …

c) The 'beyond' of God (his transcendence, the *mysterium tremendum*) is part of all authentic religious experience. On your own spiritual journey, what has made this real for you?

d) The last lines talk about 'my word', that is the Word of God, a word which comes to us in silence, in nature, through people and in the Scriptures. In this word, we are called to place our trust. The great Psalm 130 puts it like this: 'I wait for the Lord, my soul waits, and in his word I hope' (Psalm 130:5).

Prayer

Loving God, let your resplendent light illumine our darkness; speak to us and shatter our deafness! May your word penetrate our hearts and change our lives again and again.

We make our prayer through our Lord Jesus Christ, your Son, who lives and reigns with you in the unity of the Holy Spirit, God for ever and ever. Amen.

Themes across the readings

Mark's account of Jesus' immersion by John is about a terse as it could be. The following verse, exploring the interior meaning of the event, is also brief. To catch the significance we can turn to the fabulous reading from Isaiah. Here we find the deep invitation, the assurance of the faithfulness and grace of God, all explored in a series of evocative metaphors. As I reflect on my own Christian baptism into Christ's death and resurrection, Isaiah can guide me as I continue to make my own today the gift given then.

Chapter 13

Sunday in Ordinary Time 2B

Thought for the day

It is good to stop from time to time and ask myself, what am I looking for? This can be answered in the ideal: 'What do I think I *should* be looking for?' or in the real: 'What do I actually want as evidenced by my choices and actions?' To move from one to the other we need the *grace of dissatisfaction*. In the words of Augustine, 'You must be dissatisfied with the way your are now, if you ever want to get to where you are not yet' (Sermon 169).

Prayer

Shake us up, Lord, and help us to see ourselves as we truly are, often settling for less, for the moderately good and the reasonably faithful. Give us a longing for more, for all you have in store for us, and on the way bless us with exhilaration that we may be joyful bearers of your Good News. Through Christ our Lord. Amen.

🌿 Gospel 🌿

Jn 1:35 The next day John again was standing with two of his disciples, ³⁶ and as he watched Jesus walk by, he exclaimed, 'Look, here is the Lamb of God!' ³⁷ The two disciples heard him say this, and they followed Jesus. ³⁸ When Jesus turned and saw them following, he said to them, 'What are you looking for?' They said to him, 'Rabbi' (which translated means Teacher), 'where are you staying?' ³⁹ He said to them,

'Come and see.' They came and saw where he was staying, and they remained with him that day. It was about four o'clock in the afternoon. [40] One of the two who heard John speak and followed him was Andrew, Simon Peter's brother. [41] He first found his brother Simon and said to him, 'We have found the Messiah' (which is translated Anointed). [42] He brought Simon to Jesus, who looked at him and said, 'You are Simon son of John. You are to be called Cephas' (which is translated Peter).

Initial observations

In the ancient tradition, there were three 'epiphanies' after Christmas: the visit of the Magi (the Epiphany proper), the baptism in the Jordan (the voice from heaven) and the wedding feast at Cana (they saw his glory). Although we now use a three–year cycle of readings, this triple epiphany influences today's choice of John's Gospel and the acclamation of the Baptist, 'Here is the Lamb of God.' Below, greater than usual space is given to the commentary, because the text is so rich and powerful.

Kind of writing

The call stories in the Synoptic Gospels strip away all questions of human psychology and practicality, so that the sovereign voice and call of Jesus may stand out. In the Fourth Gospel, the author offers a more credible psychology of call, but again it is not history in our sense. John's Gospel uses the call stories to present a profound Christology. In this chapter one, from v. 19, Jesus is named 'one whom you do not know', the lamb of God, the Son of God, Rabbi, Messiah, 'the one about whom Moses wrote', the King of Israel, the Son of Man.

Theology drives the narrative and the apparently historical verisimilitude of human response and chain reaction is the creation of the author.

Old Testament background

The LORD said to Moses and Aaron in the land of Egypt: This month shall mark for you the beginning of months; it shall be the first month of the year for you. Tell the whole congregation of Israel that on the tenth of this month they are to take a lamb for each family, a lamb for each household. If a household is too small for a whole lamb, it shall join its closest neighbour in obtaining one; the lamb shall be divided in proportion to the number of people who eat of it. Your lamb shall be without blemish, a year-old male; you may take it from the sheep or from the goats. (Exodus 12:1–6)

New Testament foreground

The Fourth Gospel has a special outline for these days.

a. The first day: the proclamation of the Baptist (1:19–28).
b. The 'next day': John bears witness to Jesus (1:29–34)
c. The 'next day': the call of Andrew and Simon (1:35–42)
d. The 'next day': the call of Philip and Nathaniel (1:43–51)

As the following story begins 'on the third day', the author seems to have lost count or is writing with some symbolic intent. In any case, the sequence of days in chapter 1 means the chapter is to be read as a whole, given that one story gives rise immediately to the next.

(b) Passover in John: see John 2:13, 23; 6:4; 11:55; 12:1; 13:1; 18:28, 39; 19:14.

'After this, when Jesus knew that all was now finished, he said (in order to fulfil the scripture), "I am thirsty." A jar full of sour wine was standing there. So they put a sponge full of the wine on a branch of hyssop and held it to his mouth' (John 19:28–29; see Exodus 12:22). 'Since it was the day of Preparation, the Jews did not want the bodies left on the cross during the sabbath, especially because that sabbath was a day of great solemnity. So they asked Pilate to have the legs of the crucified men broken and the bodies removed. Then the soldiers came and broke the legs of the first and of the other who had been crucified with him. But when they came to Jesus and saw that he was already dead, *they did not break his legs*' (John 19:31–34; cf. Exodus 12:46 regarding the Passover lamb).

St Paul

> Clean out the old yeast so that you may be a new batch, as you really are unleavened. For our paschal lamb, Christ, has been sacrificed (1 Corinthians 5:7).

> But now apart from the law the righteousness of God (which is attested by the law and the prophets) has been disclosed – namely, the righteousness of God through the faithfulness of Jesus Christ for all who believe. For there is no distinction, for all have sinned and fall short of the glory of God. But they are justified freely by his grace through the redemption that is in Christ Jesus. *God publicly displayed him at his death as the mercy seat accessible through faith.* This was to demonstrate his righteousness, because God in his forbearance had passed over the sins previously committed. This was also to demonstrate his righteousness in the present time, so that he would be just and the justifier of the one who lives because of Jesus' faithfulness (Romans 3:21–26, NET version).

Brief commentary

(V. 35)

John's Gospel counts the days in the early part of the gospel (see above). John the Baptist has just given an oblique account of the baptism, and it is time for Jesus to call his disciples. The Baptist apparently directs two of his disciples to Jesus. This is unlikely historically, but, nevertheless it is true that the core constituency of the Johannine community was former followers of the Baptist (also Pharisees in chapter 3, Samaritans in chapter 4 and Gentiles, also in chapter 4).

(V. 36)

Note the contrast between the static John and the dynamic Jesus. The words here are the first human reaction to Jesus in John's Gospel and they are accordingly rich in resonance. Passover is a key to the structure of this Gospel, in which three Passovers are marked. The final Passover receives a very careful introduction in 13:1–4.

Furthermore, in this Gospel, the final Passover is Friday night to Saturday, not Thursday night to Friday. At the very time on Friday when the slaughter of the lambs for Passover began, Jesus is handed over by Pilate to death. This is the explanation of the otherwise puzzling timing: 'Now it was the day of Preparation for the Passover; and it was about noon' (John 19:14).

Finally, the treatment of Jesus' body after death echoes the instruction regarding the Passover lamb in Exodus 12. All in all, the acclamation of the Baptist exposes a deep vein of theological reflection.

(V. 37)
John the 'voice' has spoken. The two followers of the Baptist detach from him to follow Jesus. Who these two are we will learn in a moment.

(V. 38)
The first words of Jesus in this gospel are resonant: *what are you looking for* (lit. seeking). (i) This is a gospel of quest stories, of which this is the first. (ii) The words of the Risen Lord to Mary at the tomb resemble these words but are significantly different: *Whom are you looking for?* In a word, Jesus proclaimed a message; the first Christians proclaimed a person. The explanation of rabbi tells us the gospel was finally edited outside of Jewish territory. Rabbi is positive in this gospel (John 1:38, 49; 3:2, 26; 4:31; 6:25; 9:2; 11:8).

'Staying' (or in the older translation 'abiding') is a word of deep significance in this gospel (John 1:32–33, 38–39; 2:12; 3:36; 4:40; 5:38; 6:27, 56; 7:9; 8:31, 35; 9:41; 10:40; 11:6, 54; 12:24, 34, 46; 14:10, 17, 25; 15:4–7, 9–10, 16; 19:31; 21:22–23). One example: 'As the Father has loved me, so I have loved you; abide in my love. If you keep my commandments, you will abide in my love, just as I have kept my Father's commandments and abide in his love' (John 15:9–10). To find out where Jesus is staying/abiding it is not sufficient to have his postcode!

(V. 39)
To come and see is an invitation firstly to experience (see 1 John 1:1–4) and then to witness (1 John 1:5). It is also an invitation to the seeing of faith, an ambiguous value in this Gospel where there are two kinds of seeing. The translation of 'four o'clock' is hopelessly up-to-date! The

number ten is a figure of completion (ten plagues, ten commandments, ten males over thirteen years of age to make up a synagogue congregation, the *minyan*), and something is coming to completion here. 'Tenth hour' is much better.

(V. 40)

At last we learn who these are. The sequence is a flat contradiction of the Synoptic tradition and may reflect the Johannine reserve towards the Peter traditions. Nevertheless, it is presumed all readers/hearers know who Simon Peter is and why he is important.

(V. 41)

The proclamation is startling. In the Synoptic tradition, this confession is the fruit of experience and struggle and, furthermore, is assigned to Simon himself. By the time this gospel was written, 'Christ' is almost a personal name for Jesus.

(V. 42)

This is also a surprise. First of all, this is the only occurrence *in the gospels* of the Aramaic 'Cephas', immediately translated as Peter. Secondly, only in Matthew 16:13–20 is the change of name appended to the confession at Caesarea Philippi. There is no motive given for the change at this very early stage in John's narrative. In fact, Peter gives no reaction whatsoever at this point. Thirdly, there is a related 'confession' of Peter in typically Johannine form in 6:68–69, but no special appointment or change of name follows. All in all, an intriguing puzzle.

Pointers for prayer

a) John pointed the disciples towards Jesus as the one they should follow. Do you remember the people in your life who have pointed you in a new and life-giving direction? Perhaps in some cases this may have involved directing you away from your association with them, for example leaving home, changing jobs, etc.

b) Accepting an invitation to 'Come and see' may be part of exploring a new path in life. When has this been so for you?

Who issued you the invitation? What benefits came to you from accepting the invitation?

c) Andrew did not keep the good news to himself but also invited his brother to join him in following Jesus. What is your experience of receiving, or giving, an invitation to join in some worthwhile venture?

e) Jesus looked at Peter and could see what he would become. Who have been the people who have been able to name for you your potential? For whom have you been able to do this?

Prayer

From our earliest days, O God, you call us by name. Make our ears attentive to your voice, our spirits eager to respond, so that, having heard you in Jesus your anointed one, we may draw others to be his disciples.

We ask this through our Lord Jesus Christ, your Son, who lives and reigns with you in the unity of the Holy Spirit, God for ever and ever. Amen.

🌿 Second Reading 🌿

1 Cor 6:12 *'All things are lawful for me '– but not everything is beneficial. 'All things are lawful for me' – but I will not be controlled by anything.* ¹³ 'Food is for the stomach and the stomach is for food, but God will do away with both.' The body is not for sexual immorality, but for the Lord, and the Lord for the body. ¹⁴ Now God indeed raised the Lord and he will raise us by his power. ¹⁵ Do you not know that your bodies are members of Christ? Should I take the members of Christ and make them members of a prostitute? Never! ¹⁶ *Or do you not know that anyone who is united with a prostitute is one body with her? For it is said, 'The two will become one flesh.'* ¹⁷ But the one united with the Lord is one spirit with him. ¹⁸ Flee sexual immorality! 'Every sin a person commits is outside of the body'– but the immoral person sins against his own body. ¹⁹ Or do you not know that your body is the temple of the Holy Spirit who is in you, whom you have from God, and you are not your own? [20] For you were bought at a price. Therefore glorify God with your body.

Initial observations

Within and outside of faith, sexuality remains an issue of intense interest and debate. There is not a lot of direct teaching on sexual morality in the New Testament, much of it found in these chapters in St Paul. The apostle was obliged to speak about it because of the attitudes and practices of the Corinthians. The full section runs from v. 12 to v. 20. It might be clearer to read the full version because the Lectionary excerpt, beginning with v.13b, is missing the motive behind the argument, making it harder to understand. It is obvious why v. 16 – restored here – is omitted in the lectionary.

Kind of writing

This is deliberative rhetoric, as St Paul tries to change the minds of some Corinthians. In it, he cites *slogans* of the different parties (noticed in inverted commas). He argues – from faith in the resurrection and from Scriptures – for the integrity of bodily and spiritual existence. Rhetorical questions enliven the argument. Finally, he brings into the argument his theology of the Holy Spirit and salvation. Although very brief, this 'proof' is penetrating and deep.

Origin of the reading

Corinth had a name at the time for sexual licence, but perhaps unjustly because the city was really no different from other places in the empire. The ancient world, in contrast to ours, did not directly connect religion and ethics. In this, they resemble some people today. Sex outside of and before marriage was countenanced for males only, however they managed that. At this point in the letter, Paul responds to a number of issues, as follows:

Sexual immorality: 5:1–8, 9–13

Lawsuits among believers: 6:1–11

Glorifying God in your body: 6:12–20

Related passages

> Do you not know that you are God's temple and that God's Spirit dwells in you? If anyone destroys God's temple, God will destroy that person. For God's temple is holy, and you are that temple. (1 Corinthians 3:16–17)

> You were bought with a price; do not become slaves of human masters. (1 Corinthians 7:23)

> 'All things are lawful,' but not all things are beneficial. 'All things are lawful,' but not all things build up. Do not seek your own advantage, but that of the other. (1 Corinthians 10:23–24)

Brief commentary

(V. 12)

Ancient documents did not use inverted commas. It is, nevertheless, virtually certain that Paul is citing slogans and the opinions *of others*. Paul is very much for freedom but at the same time for the correct use of freedom.

(V. 13)

The translation used here is the NET (not the usual NRSV). This is because it makes more sense to extend the inverted commas to include the phrase 'but God will do away with both'. Apparently, some had argued (i) that sex, like hunger, is a natural appetite to be satisfied without moral risk; (ii) that the body doesn't matter anyway because we will be spiritual in the world to come. The first argument responds to (ii). The body is not irrelevant: it is *for the Lord*. Here and elsewhere, Paul rejects any kind of dualism.

(V. 14)

Paul argues for an Easter ethic: the body matters because Jesus was raised from the dead and we will be too.

(V. 15)

Rhetorical questions touch the mind and the heart. Food satisfies the stomach but sexual intercourse in and of itself involves the whole person.

(V. 16)

Paul calls on the book of Genesis to make his point about the integrity of the sex act: *Therefore a man leaves his father and his mother and clings to his wife, and they become one flesh* (Genesis 2:24).

(V. 17)

Building on the previous image of union (one flesh), Paul points out that Christians are one flesh/spirit with Christ. To involve yourself in casual sexual activity is to involve Christ as well.

(V. 18)

Beginning with an exhortation, Paul once more cites a slogan, a very telling one. Even if some other sins may be materially 'outside' the body (and therefore irrelevant?), this is absolutely not the case with sexual sin. The sinner sins against himself or herself – an argument from self-regard and interest.

(V. 19)

This important image of the temple – significant elsewhere in Paul – is brought to bear ethically here. Because each of us is a member of the body of Christ and each of us is a temple of the Holy Spirit, a distinctive ethic integrating the whole person is demanded.

(V. 20)

The cultural reference here is to manumission, the setting free of slaves. We have been set free, and let us remain free and thus glory in the grace of God in Christ.

Pointers for prayer

a) The good use of hard-won freedom can be a challenge in many spheres of life. How do I manage?

b) Paul argues for oneness of the human person – what I do is who I am. In my own journey of integration, where do I find myself?

c) Paul does not argue from social custom but rather against it. What are the sources of your morality?

Prayer

God of all gifts, you love us enough to love the whole human being, all that I am. Help me to respond to your love with my whole self, not less than everything, that you may glorified and I may flourish and be fully alive. Through Christ our Lord. Amen.

🌿 First Reading 🌿

1 Sam 3:3 Samuel was lying down in the temple of the LORD, where the ark of God was. ⁴ Then the LORD called, 'Samuel! Samuel!' and he said, 'Here I am!' ⁵ and ran to Eli, and said, 'Here I am, for you called me.' But he said, 'I did not call; lie down again.' So he went and lay down. ⁶ The LORD called again, 'Samuel!' Samuel got up and went to Eli, and said, 'Here I am, for you called me.' But he said, 'I did not call, my son; lie down again.' ⁷ Now Samuel did not yet know the LORD, and the word of the LORD had not yet been revealed to him. ⁸ The LORD called Samuel again, a third time. And he got up and went to Eli, and said, 'Here I am, for you called me.' Then Eli perceived that the LORD was calling the boy. ⁹ Therefore Eli said to Samuel, 'Go, lie down; and if he calls you, you shall say, 'Speak, LORD, for your servant is listening.'' So Samuel went and lay down in his place. ¹⁰ Now the LORD came and stood there, calling as before, 'Samuel! Samuel!' And Samuel said, 'Speak, for your servant is listening.'

1 Sam 3:19 As Samuel grew up, the LORD was with him and let none of his words fall to the ground.

Initial observations

For a better grasp of the context, all of 1 Samuel 1–2 should also be read. Samuel was the prophet in ancient Israel who anointed Saul as their first king. Today's reading is the story of his call as a prophet, the foundation of his ministry. The call of Samuel – quite dramatic – makes a good match with the call stories in today's gospel.

Kind of writing

This is a call story, but an unusual one, in the form of a 'commissioning report'. Examples could be Isaiah 6; Jeremiah 1:4–10; Ezekiel 1:1–3:15. The typical features include a *dialogue* in which God calls a prophet. Initially, there is some objection or hesitation, followed by an affirmation of the call, which then leads to the mission of the prophet. These features are present here but *obliquely*, as signified by the slowness in realising what is happening. It is a kind of acoustic 'vision' (cf. again Isaiah 6, Jeremiah 1:11–13; Ezekiel 1:1–3:15 etc.). As in stories of epiphanies, the reader is informed ahead of the characters and knows more than they do. The attention of the reader is not on *who* is speaking (we know that already) but on *how* the recipients will come to recognise the speaker. Suspense is created by having Eli come to the realisation first, although Samuel is the recipient.

Origin of the reading

The present form of the great narrative arc from Joshua to 2 Kings is deeply marked by two, much later, moments. (i) The reform undertaken in the seventh century BC, in the time of Josiah, was the first, and (ii) the second was the Deuteronomistic reform, which crystallised during the Exile around 550 BC. 1 Samuel begins the great story, with the miraculous birth and calling of the prophet. In effect, Samuel is presented as a kind of transitional figure, combining the roles of prophet, priest and judge (in the Old Testament sense). Part of the agenda concerns the demise of the priest Eli and his sons. Eli thinks Hannah is drunk, while in reality she is in anguished prayer. He is the one, in chapter 3, who by being deaf to God barely manages in his role as mentor to the boy Samuel. After this shaky start, Samuel becomes a real spokesman for God, as we can see in 1 Samuel 3:20–21.

Related passages

Here I am is found as a response to God's call: Abraham (Genesis 22:1, 11); Jacob (Genesis 31:11; 42:6); Moses (Exodus 3:4); Isaiah (Isaiah 6:8); Mary (Luke 2:38) etc.

Brief commentary

(V. 3)
The call story is a fulfilment of an oracle (1 Samuel 2:27–36). Samuel is resting very close to the Holy of Holies, the location of the most sacred object in the Temple, the ark of God.

(V. 4)
The response of Samuel is the correct one at the very start. The 'error' lies in not recognising the source of the voice, on account of his innocence and perhaps also on account of his humility.

(V. 5)
A kind of serious comedy unfolds. The priest, official communicator with God, is asleep and 'deaf', while the trainee is awake and alert. The sleeping priest recommends sleep, at first, which is at least consistent.

(V. 6)
In folk stories, you have the 'rule of three'. Something happens, it is repeated verbatim (as here) to create a pattern, so that at the third occurrence the pattern is varied and a breakthrough occurs (as here). In a fatherly way, Eli this time calls Samuel 'my son.'

(V. 7)
Samuel himself is excused by these verses – he simply had not yet experienced the Lord. The reader is reminded emphatically that the ominous absence of God at the top of the chapter (1 Samuel 3:1) was about to come to an end.

(V. 8)
On the third occurrence, Eli at last comes to insight and discernment.

(V. 9)
The advice of Eli is resonant and powerful: *Speak, Lord, for your servant is listening.*

(V. 10)
This is rather more than a voice: 'The Lord came and stood there'. Samuel omits the address Lord, as recommended by Eli, perhaps from a

sense of awe. (The next few verses are left out in the lectionary, because the demise of Eli and his sons would distract from the purpose of the reading today.)

(V. 19)

The translation here is a little ambiguous on account of the use of 'his.' It means the Lord fulfilled the prophecies of Samuel, and as a result his 'words did not fall to the ground'. In 1 Samuel 3:19–4:1, Samuel is confirmed very fully as a prophet in God's sight.

Pointers for prayer

a) The story may remind us of times in our own lives when we were asleep and deaf to God. What was that experience like? How did we come out of that state? Was there some person or event, of special significance?

b) 'You called, shouted, broke through my deafness; you flared, blazed, banished my blindness; you lavished your fragrance, I gasped and now I pant for you; I tasted you, and I hunger and thirst; you touched me, and I burned for your peace.' Augustine, *Confessions* 10:27.28.

c) The great discernment at the centre of the story lies in the words: 'Speak, Lord, for your servant is listening.' It is a very open prayer, unreserved and unconditional. Have I prayed such a prayer and what difference has it made?

Prayer

Loving God, often we are asleep and deaf, distracted by the cares of life and 'the desire for other things.' Speak to us, Lord, your servants are listening: may your word penetrate our hearts and continue to change our lives. Through Christ our Lord. Amen.

Themes across the readings

The gospel recounts two call stories. The first is quite like our first reading: just as Eli directed Samuel to the Lord, John directs his disciples to Jesus. The sense of both discovery and discernment continues in the second part of gospel, when Andrew draws his brother to the Messiah. In both the first reading and in the gospel, there is a marked receptivity and openness to the call of God.

Soli Deo Gloria!

Exploring the Prophets

As you might expect, there is a vast literature on the biblical prophets and it would not be possible (or even wise) to attempt an exhaustive reading list.

1. Recommendations

Jewish Authors

    Nahum Ward–Lev, *The Liberating Path of the Hebrew Prophets: Then and Now*. New York: Orbis, 2019.

    Abraham Heschel, *The Prophets*, New York: HarperPerennial, 2001.

Christian Authors

    Walter Brueggemann, *The Prophetic Imagination* (40th anniversary edition). Minneapolis: Fortress Press, 2018.

    Carol J. Dempsey, *The Prophets: A Liberation – Critical Reading*. Minneapolis: Augsburg Fortress, 2000.

The book by Walter Brueggemann has become a modern classic. He continues to write, reflect and apply the insights of the prophets to contemporary issues.

    Walter Brueggemann, *Virus as a Summons to Faith. Biblical Reflections in a Time of Loss, Grief and Uncertainty*. Foreword by Nahum Ward–Lev. Eugene, OR: Cascade Books, 2020.

On Isaiah specifically, this is an approachable book, written from a Christian perspective:

    John Goldingay, *Isaiah for Everyone*. London: SPCK, 2015.

2. The use of the Old Testament in Year B
(Feasts and Sundays, including any optional readings).

Statistics can yield surprises. In the Lectionary, there is relative neglect of the last three books of the Pentateuch, most of the historical books and the Wisdom books. By contrast, Genesis (8), Exodus (6) and the Prophets (32) are given a privileged place, being especially important from Advent to the Baptism and from Lent to Pentecost, in other words for the most important Christian high holidays. Within that scheme, Isaiah has been given far and away the lion's share. It would be hard to celebrate Advent, Christmas, Lent, Holy Week and the Easter Vigil without this extraordinary text. If in doubt, a glance at the biblical index to this book should settle the question!

Pentateuch (21 readings)

Genesis: Holy Family (B); Lent 1, 2; Easter Vigil 1; 2; Pentecost Vigil (1); Sunday 10, 27.

Exodus: Lent 3; Holy Thursday; Easter Vigil 3; Pentecost Vigil (2); Corpus Christi; Sunday 18.

Leviticus: Sunday 6.

Numbers: Sunday 26.

Deuteronomy: Sunday 4, 9, 22, 31, Holy Trinity.

Historical books (7 readings)

Joshua: Sunday 21.

1 Samuel: Sunday 2.

2 Samuel: Advent 4.

1 Kings: Sunday 19, 32.

2 Kings: Sunday 17.

2 Chronicles: Lent 4.

Wisdom books (8 readings)

Job: Sunday 5, 12.

Proverbs: Sunday 20.

Wisdom: Sunday 13, 25, 28.

Sirach: Holy Family; Christmas 2.

Prophets (32 readings, of which 18 are from Isaiah)

Isaiah: Advent 1, 2, 3; Christmas Day 1, 2, 3, 4; Epiphany; Baptism; Baptism (B); Palm Sunday; Good Friday; Easter Vigil 4, 5; Sunday 7, 23, 24, 29.

Jeremiah: Lent 5; Sunday 16, 30.

Baruch: Easter Vigil 6.

Ezekiel: Easter Vigil 7; Pentecost Vigil (3); Sunday 11, 14.

Daniel: Sunday 33, 34.

Hosea: Sunday 8.

Joel: Pentecost Vigil (4).

Amos: Sunday 15.

Jonah: Sunday 3.

Biblical Index

The index follows the order of Old Testament books as found in Catholic bibles; the chapter and verse numbering follows the NRSV.

Other ancient sources

Other writers